Robert Van de Weyer was for many yea... economics, specializing in economic pl... economics (on which he has written t.... ....d monetary economics. In 1976 he won the Adam Smith Prize for young economists, and in 1986 he won the Winifred Mary Stanbrook Book Prize for *Wickwyn: A Vision of the Future* (SPCK). Since 1982 he has been an Anglican priest, serving a village in Cambridgeshire. He is a prolific author on both religious and economic themes.

To
Babu Patwardhan, who first alerted me to
the ill effects of usury

AGAINST USURY

Resolving the Economic, Ecological and Welfare Crisis

Robert Van de Weyer

First published in Great Britain in 2010

Society for Promoting Christian Knowledge
36 Causton Street
London SW1P 4ST

The author and publisher have made every effort to ensure that the external website and
email addresses included in this book are correct and up to date at the time of going to
press. The author and publisher are not responsible for the content, quality or continuing
accessibility of the sites.

British Library Cataloguing-in-Publication Data
A catalogue record for this book is available from the British Library

ISBN 978–0–281–06210–2

1 3 5 7 9 10 8 6 4 2

Typeset by Graphicraft Limited, Hong Kong
Printed in Great Britain by Ashford Colour Press

Produced on paper from sustainable forests

Contents

Contents

Contents

Foreword by Professor Philip Booth

Editorial and Programme Director
Institute of Economic Affairs

———•◆•———

Robert Van de Weyer's thesis is that usury is at the root of most of the serious problems that society faces. He defines usury, not in the way that is commonly understood, but as the unequal sharing of risk by two parties. Van de Weyer makes the case that this is the historically correct definition of usury. It explains why, for example, in Islamic financial arrangements equity finance is permissible (because the lender is bearing the risks) but a fixed interest loan is not generally permissible. In the case of a fixed interest arrangement the borrower bears the risk of failure and gets the benefits from success but the lender obtains a fixed return. The author then goes on to suggest that a lot of the problems within the financial system have arisen as a result of the unequal sharing of risks in this way.

The author is certainly right to highlight this issue. Governments throughout the world have done everything they can to crucify equity interests (or company shares) whereby the investor directly bears the risks of investment projects. Equity interests in companies are substantially over-taxed compared with fixed-interest investments, and often the returns to equity are taxed twice or three times. Indeed, this is one of the main explanations for the existence of so-called tax havens, which ensure that equity returns are only taxed once. Furthermore, the regulation of insurance companies and pension funds in recent years has made it more and more difficult for these entities to take equity risks in their investment policies. Members of defined benefit pension funds, who used to bear some of the risks of low returns, have now, as a result of legislation, pushed that risk on to sponsoring companies. Relating this problem specifically to the financial crash, it is clear that one reason for the gearing and excessive risk taking of the investment banks was the tax treatment of equity investments. This made banks ever-more keen to create new packages and methods of gearing that were constructed out of fixed interest lending. Indeed, as the author points out, the very existence of high general tax rates discourages the taking of equity risks because the Treasury gains from the success that comes from equity risks but does not lose from the failure: all income and capital taxes, by their nature, tax success. Taking these points together, we can say that the government creates an environment that actively encourages the form of usury that the author describes.

How should we deal with this problem? Firstly, the author would like to see much lower rates of tax, partly resulting from his other proposals discussed below. However, even in a lower-tax environment and in non-discriminatory tax systems, it is likely that usury would develop as a result of voluntary decisions. But, again, these voluntary decisions are distorted by the ability of banks to minimise the amount of liquid assets they hold against deposits, and by the use of deposit insurance systems that allow depositors to impose the risks of their financial decisions on the deposit insurance system and, in the last resort, on the taxpayer. This can be regarded as 'involuntary usury'. Banks take individuals' deposits of money and are able to lend them out to borrowers as if the deposits were long-term capital investments knowing that, if the risks they are taking are too great, they would be 'bailed out' directly or indirectly by the taxpayer.

The solution to this, argues Van de Weyer, is, more or less, to separate the investment side from the deposit-taking side of banks' activities. The money that we hold for everyday financial transactions would be kept in 'deposit banks'. The capital that we accumulate for longer-term saving would be kept in 'capital banks'. The activities of the latter would not need to be surrounded by detailed regulation (and investors would be aware that their capital was at risk), but the former would be limited in their activities so that cash was always available to repay deposits on demand.

This proposal is controversial in the free-market circles of the Institute of Economic Affairs (IEA). Tim Congdon, for example, has made a very strong case against what are some-times called 'narrow banking' models similar to those proposed by the author. Many 'Austrian' economists, on the other hand, would approve. Some would believe that the proposals of the author would come about in a financial system that was com-pletely unregulated by the state; others have suggested that such a system should be brought about by legislation. The advantage of the separation of investment and deposit banking, argue its free-market proponents, is that it creates a case for a very specific regulatory framework but allows financial institutions to operate very freely within that framework.

This is a debate that will continue, and the author's highly original contribution is very welcome. It is certainly preferable to the mass of commentary on the tedious debate within the European Union about how to extend the tentacles of detailed regulation into those parts of the financial system (hedge funds and so on) which, in fact, had nothing to do with the financial crash. The author's ability both to circumnavigate that debate and relate a much more pertinent debate to an important discourse on the meaning of usury is laudatory.

The author also relates the concept of usury to a much wider range of situations. For example, he discusses the issue of global warming. Perhaps it is the second biggest economic issue in most people's thoughts, after the financial crash.

The author suggests outlawing CO_2 production at a pre-announced future date. It is arguable that the production of CO_2 by one person causes harm to another so, perhaps, a case could be made that we should ban it. But perhaps there is another way here. As the economist Graham Dawson has suggested, there is no reason why the production of CO_2 should not be treated as a potential tort. A collective action application for an injunction or compensation could be taken out and the science (and the extent of damage) could be argued out in court. After all, there is little point in making the production of CO_2 a criminal offence if it does not harm anybody. If it does harm somebody then we have a perfectly good legal mechanism (especially in the UK) for dealing with this matter. Nevertheless, the author's analysis that pollution (and CO_2 production) should be intrinsically regarded as a problem of one party imposing costs and risks on others without them having any say in the matter at least gets us arguing about the appropriate measures to take. As is so often the case in this book, the author's points are inter-related (his approach is 'holistic' in today's management jargon). High taxes especially penalise high-risk investments because the state gains from progressive taxation of profits but does not share in the losses of investment projects. 'Green' technologies are especially high risk and speculative. Our tax system therefore particularly penalises 'green' technologies. Would the railways ever have been built in an economy that taxes profits remitted as dividends to individuals at a rate of close to 60%? Perhaps not.

The author's conclusions about taxes and the welfare state are particularly pertinent. Whilst much ink has been spilt on the financial crash – and the political class has made much political capital from it – that same political class is largely silent about the moral hazard caused by taxation and the welfare state. Despite the lessons of history, and lessons from abroad, there is still little serious discussion amongst politicians about the need for much lower taxes and the desirability of individuals, families and communities taking charge, once again, of their own health and welfare arrangements. The author suggests one way in which we could move in that direction, whilst emphasizing, of course, the moral hazard and unequal sharing of risks that come from tax-financed and government planned provision for potentially insurable risks. Returning health and welfare insurance to the individual, the family and to civil society, using commercial and semi-commercial organisations, in the way that the author suggests, would be hugely beneficial. The poor would be protected through having their contributions to providers financed through taxation. Others would take responsibility for themselves within a structure that was simultaneously paternalistic but largely voluntary.

This is a thoughtful and important book. In some places it will be regarded as idiosyncratic. Without that combination I am sure that the author would not have received commendations from the Archbishop of Canterbury, Tony Benn and the Editorial Director of the IEA! There is no harm, of course, in taking risks with thought experiments; many useful ideas come out of idiosyncratic thinking and the author should be congratulated on this as well as his careful scholarship and original thinking in the field of Christian social thought. We have hopefully now finished with the debate on liberation theology and the need for revolution to overthrow 'sinful' structures. It would be nice to think that we are also coming to the end of the era of Christians responding to every economic problem by suggesting that the state should raise taxation or pass a law to directly address all that we dislike in society. The author is, by no means, taking a libertarian position, but he does propose returning financial decision making and welfare provision to the community. We can argue about the details of the author's proposals but how can Christians, over the past two generations, have so comprehensively misunderstood the legitimate role of political authority? It is to be hoped that this book will help push Christian social thinking in a much more fruitful direction.

Foreword by Tarek El Diwany

Consultant on Islamic Finance
Author of The Problem with Interest

———————•◦•◆•◦•———————

As a boy, I spent a school holiday with my mother in what was then the German Democratic Republic. She was born near Leipzig in the 1930s and had remained there until her escape to the West some 20 years later. Our home for those few weeks was a small town, unchanged for centuries it seemed, except for the backdrop of identical grey apartment blocks on the nearby hills. These spoke of central planning and hatred for life on a human scale. One evening we sat in a smoke-filled lounge enjoying the supplies of coffee and chocolate that had arrived with my mother. 'Which is better,' an old man asked me in front of the assembled guests, '*communismus oder capitalismus*?' '*Capitalismus*,' I replied gleefully.

But of course I was wrong. It is clear to me now that communism and capitalism have failed the world in ways that are approximately as bad as one another. Though generations of students have faced a seemingly stark choice of value system, in practice these two thoroughfares of political economy have led to precisely the same destination: a land in which the masses toil for the benefit of a small elite.

While communism exercised its power through such blatant injustices as the confiscation of assets, the instruments of capitalism have tended to work more subtly and have therefore remained largely beyond the public conscience. Chief among these is the practice of usury. Though rarely scrutinised by the modern economist, its destructive power has not lessened since the best minds of Greece and Rome denounced it. Today its casualties include the children of Africa and the rainforests of the Amazon, both despoiled in the effort to service foreign debt. Among its allies is a culture of debt-finance that has spawned massive global corporations and led to a debasement of daily life even in the rich world. The artisans who built the charming villages of England have been replaced by a few monolithic building companies whose bequest to future generations is a landscape of characterless housing estates. Gone too are the small shopkeepers of the local town, their business usurped by out-of-town monopolies that call themselves supermarkets. Never was the word 'market' used so inappropriately. Life is being cheapened, variety is diminishing, and control is being centralised. Isn't this what communism did to Eastern Germany?

In these times of financial crisis, people of religious faith have an opportunity to show the world that there really is a third way of organizing our economic affairs. Such efforts will inevitably bring the crime of usury back into the public conscience for this is a central part of our common prophetic heritage. Of the various forms of usury that are defined in Islam, the usury of loans is nowadays the most widely practised. It is therefore my pleasure to support a work that addresses this form of usury and seeks to understand the rationale for its prohibition. Such discussions have become all the more critical in the face of attempts by practitioners of usury to ignore or underplay it as an issue. While not all of the ideas expressed here will accord with the juristic position in Islam, we remain united on the central theme before us. 'Even if usury is much, it always leads to utter poverty,' said the prophet Muhammad, peace be upon him. From this it is clear that the issue of usury cannot be ignored for ever. It will either be resolved by force of argument, or by force of circumstance when the people have nothing left to eat.

Preface

The line of thinking explored in this book began for me on a dusty road in central India in June 1969. I was on a long hike when I encountered an elderly man called Babu Patwardhan. A long-standing follower of Mahatma Gandhi – and looking remarkably like the Mahatma in both dress and visage – Babu Patwardhan now wandered from village to village promoting an idea he called 'Chalanashuddhi'. This in essence is a means of reordering the economic system to abolish usury; he argued that it is the only means of realizing Gandhi's vision of an economy that provides for welfare and work for everyone, and functions in harmony with the natural environment.

Babu Patwardhan also gave in the course of our long conversation a remarkable exposition of the teachings of Jesus Christ, relating them to the Hindu philosophy of Advaita Vedanta. That exposition helped me towards my eventual conversion to Christianity 18 months later; I have also come to see a link between Advaita Vedanta and the abolition of usury – a link which I address briefly at the end of this book.

Babu Patwardhan gave me a copy of the book he had written two years earlier entitled *Chalanashuddhi*, in which he presented his ideas in detail. I still treasure that copy; and I dedicate this book to his memory.

As the years have passed, the issues addressed by Babu Patwardhan have become more and more serious, not only in rural India but across the world. I have no compunction in saying that they now constitute a trio of crises. And it is to Babu Patwardhan that I owe the insight that these crises form a single crisis, with the same underlying cause, and with connected solutions. If this present book has any merit, it is in amplifying this insight with ideas drawn from elsewhere, from the religious traditions and from the history of economic thought.

I hope the whole of this book engages readers' interest. I hope too that, where I bring economic theories to bear, I have emulated the example of the great economists from the past, such as Adam Smith and John Maynard Keynes, in their simplicity and clarity of exposition. Also, so as not to interrupt the flow of argument, I have added an Epilogue, giving the intellectual background to key ideas.

Nonetheless I feel diffident about inviting people to read an entire book of ideas and proposals from start to finish, albeit that the subject matter could hardly be more important. So those pressed for time might confine themselves to the Prologue and the Anti-Usury Manifesto that forms Chapter 5 – and then dip into earlier chapters as the Manifesto indicates and as they feel inclined.

I wish to express my gratitude to Professor Philip Booth of the Institute of Economic Affairs and to Tarek El Diwany, a distinguished expert on Islamic finance, for their very helpful comments during the writing of this book – and also for their Forewords. Needless to say, all the book's errors and shortcomings are entirely my own.

Although my own reflections on usury date from an encounter with a Hindu, it is in the scriptures and later writings of Judaism, Christianity and Islam that one finds the most trenchant opposition to usurious practices of various kinds – with usury presented as the primary economic sin. The titles of the first four chapters are in Hebrew and Arabic, as well as English, to reflect this religious background.

Robert Van de Weyer
robert@vandeweyer.co.uk

Prologue

———◆·◆·◆———

1 Ecology

In 1798, Thomas Robert Malthus, who was both a priest and an economist, wrote an essay, which brought him great fame, predicting ecological catastrophe. He expressed the belief in *An Essay on the Principle of Population* that the human population would always tend to grow faster than the capacity of the earth to provide food for it. So even if the Industrial Revolution, then in its infancy, was able to provide more goods to consume, the planet itself placed limits on the degree to which the economy could grow.

In the following century and a half the expansion of the global economy seemed to disprove this gloomy prediction. Vast tracts of the Americas, Asia, Australia and Africa were successively brought under the plough, or turned into plantations or ranches. In addition farming methods improved, steadily increasing the harvests. As a result the burgeoning populations of Britain and the other industrial countries remained well-fed.

But in the 1930s an English amateur meteorologist, G. S. Callendar, began to warn of another way in which the human population was pressing on the limits of the planet. In letters and notebooks he analysed how emissions of carbon dioxide from fossil fuels were beginning to create a 'greenhouse effect' that would eventually cause the earth's climate to become substantially hotter. Although in his lifetime Callendar was largely ignored, in the years following his death in 1964 people became aware of various other ways in which human activity was upsetting the ecology of the planet. From the 1980s fears about

1

climate change also began to grow, until by the turn of the millennium these fears were gripping the public consciousness.

At a technical level there is little argument about what needs to be done to avert global warming. As a matter of urgency we must develop technologies that can generate energy without emitting greenhouse gases – and hence without using fossil fuels. Moreover, it seems likely that green technologies might, with sufficient research, be cheaper than using oil and coal. Yet during the past two or three decades investment in the development of green technologies has been pitiful, and the results have been correspondingly meagre.

Malthus offered no means of avoiding the ecological catastrophe he foresaw. He hoped that priests like himself, when young couples came to arrange their weddings, would offer a short homily on the dangers of over-population, and urge them to practise sexual abstinence. But he thought it more likely that humanity would soon be haunted by chronic famine, leading to warfare and disease. As the present generation contemplates the fate of its grandchildren and great-grandchildren, it can't help fearing that Malthus will at last be vindicated.

2 Economics

In 1820 Malthus made a second prediction, claiming in *Principles of Political Economy* that industrial economies have an inherent tendency towards depression. He lamented the high level of unemployment in Britain following the end of the Napoleonic Wars, and feared that this would be normal in peacetime. The reason was that the new middle classes, who were making their fortunes from industry, tended to save excessively, in their desire to achieve financial security and to accumulate wealth for their heirs. While they invested some of these savings in new factories, much of it was hoarded as gold and silver coins. This represented a continuous drain of demand from the economy, throwing people out of work.

In the following century the enormous expansion of world trade seemed to prove Malthus wrong. As Britain, followed by the rest of the Western world, opened up shipping routes to Asia and then to Africa, demand for goods manufactured in Western factories grew sufficiently to keep the machines humming. There were periodic depressions, but the global economy always bounced back into boom.

However, in the 1920s the industrial countries at last sank into a depression that, left to itself, threatened to become permanent, with unemployment in some places rising to a third of the workforce. The dominant economist of the period, John Maynard Keynes, argued that Malthus' prediction was at last being fulfilled; and he developed an overarching theory to explain this. In *The General Theory of Employment, Interest and Money* (1936), he urged governments to compensate for excessive private savings by public profligacy, spending more than they raised in taxation – and borrowing the difference. But he recognized that such measures could only be temporary, since governments who borrow continually, like households, eventually become insolvent. So he regarded 'secular stagnation' as the natural state of modern economies.

Once again, however, events seemed to disprove such fears. Hitler's war and the subsequent reconstruction caused government borrowing to balloon; and persistent inflation, rising to over 20 per cent in the mid 1970s, eroded the debt, enabling governments to borrow more. Then rapid industrialization in Asia boosted demand for Western goods. As they grew richer, Asians saved a very high proportion of their incomes, threatening depression. But by the mid 1990s this money was finding its way through the global banking system to Western families, who used much of it to buy more housing than they needed – larger houses in which to live, plus second homes elsewhere. As house prices surged, Western families came to regard their houses as their pensions, and so they virtually gave up saving. The global economy thus enjoyed the longest boom in history.

But the housing bubble could not last. When it began to burst in 2007, it also brought the global banking system to the point of collapse, saved only by massive government support. And, following the bursting of the bubble, it was inevitable that Western families would resume their normal patterns of saving. Combined with Asian savings, this would inevitably threaten the global economy with stagnation.

Perhaps there will be more warfare, civil or international, or some other disaster, that may stimulate massive public borrowing, followed by prolonged inflation as the only means for governments to remain solvent. Or perhaps there will in due course be other housing bubbles, creating an illusory boom in the global economy. And there will continue to be cyclical forces that will push economies upwards from time to time. Yet, if Malthus and Keynes are right, these upswings are likely to be modest and short. In the absence of wars and bubbles, the economic future appears bleak.

3 Welfare

Malthus, along with many others, soon realized that his predictions on ecology and economics had important implications for social welfare. As the population rose faster than food supplies, food prices would rise; and as the economy stagnated, many families would not be able to earn sufficient wages to feed themselves. So there would be growing pressure on national and local governments to provide financial support. Yet, economic stagnation would depress tax revenues; and, since any support would be spent on food, it would push up food prices still further.

Some, including an archbishop of Canterbury, favoured withdrawing every kind of support for the poor, arguing that this would limit the population to the level that could both find work and feed itself. In fact, the British government abolished support to families in their own homes, and instead instituted a national system of workhouses whose material standards were deliberately set so low that only people in the most desperate need would enter them. Other Western countries, as they industrialized, followed the British example.

During the course of the twentieth century wages in the industrialized countries rose quickly. Meanwhile the political franchise was extended to the entire adult population, so governments needed the support of the poor as well as the rich. As a result governments replaced workhouses with direct payments to the unemployed, the sick and the elderly, also providing education for the young and healthcare for everyone. They financed this social welfare through progressive taxation, in which tax rates rise with income, so that most people received more from the government than they paid.

But by the 1980s a number of politicians and economists were questioning this pact with voters. On the one hand, as people grew richer and lived longer, so their demands rose faster than the revenues from taxation. On the other hand, if governments raised tax rates further, they would suppress economic activity to such an extent that tax revenues would fall. However, suggestions for reform have generally been greeted with such howls of popular protest that their proponents have drawn back.

The consequence is that social welfare is chronically short of funds. And as the economy stagnates, so this shortage will grow worse. Here too Malthus seems at last to have been proved right.

4 Morality

There is no shortage of moral passion aimed at our ecological, economic and welfare crises, and religious leaders are often at the forefront of its expression. So most Christians in the West, as well as many of other faiths, are aghast at the destruction we are wreaking on God's earth; they abhor unemployment as an affront to human dignity, as well as a grave injustice; they are appalled at the poor standards of our schools and hospitals. And they call for these wrongs to be righted.

But this is the morality of ends – of what the aims of ecological, economic and social policy should be. The question is whether there is also a morality of means – a morality that would lead us from our present condition towards those ends.

In the Jewish, Christian and Islamic traditions there is a particular practice that is regarded as the primary economic sin, namely usury. There are various definitions of usury; in this book I shall define usury as the unequal allocation of risk, which incorporates all the other definitions. In the scriptures of those traditions, and in the later writings of their scholars, usury appears as the underlying cause of most economic problems; its eradication is their solution.

To the modern mind the word 'usury' seems archaic, conjuring up images of medieval money-lenders charging exorbitant interest. Yet it is striking that, in current debates about our three crises, problems in dealing with risk are central. Thus, for example, the ecological crisis arises from our collective failure to respond to the risks to our planet of atmospheric pollution – which in turn arises from our unwillingness to put our money at risk in developing green technologies. Western banks collapsed into insolvency in 2008 because, in the words of many expert commentators, they 'mis-priced' risk. And when economists consider raising taxation to pay for better welfare, a central concern is the effect of higher tax rates on the willingness of entrepreneurs to take risks. At the very least this suggests we should look again at why usury was so repugnant to our forbears.

In fact, it is the contention of this book that usury, in three different forms, is the underlying cause of all three crises, and that the different forms interact to make the crises worse. Thus the abolition, or at least the reduction, of usury provides the solutions.

When medieval writers such as Thomas Aquinas considered usury, they made clear that they were addressing a moral issue;

but they tended to use arguments that we today would regard as economic. To anyone familiar with the writings of Adam Smith, the founding father of modern economics, this is not surprising. Smith was first and foremost a moral philosopher; and in his first great book, *The Theory of Moral Sentiments* (1759), he outlined how human beings define their purposes. Then in *The Wealth of Nations* (1776) he analysed the means by which they achieve those purposes within the public arena. Thus for Smith the subject matter of economics is the morality of means.

We should follow the example of Aquinas and Smith in using mainly economic arguments in making the case against usury, and thence in showing how the triple crises can be resolved. We should also emulate them in their style of argument. Modern economic analysis tends to be couched in elaborate mathematical models. Yet these can so bedazzle our minds that we become blind to the assumptions on which they rest. Indeed, it was this blindness that prevented the great majority of economists from foreseeing the crash of 2007/08. Good economics requires no more – and no less – than careful logic and respect for facts, plus common sense about human nature.

5 Politics

When the early socialists, at the outset of the industrial era two centuries ago, began to campaign against the prevailing economic system, they were inspired by moral zeal. And, although they rarely used the term, the focus of their zeal was usury – as R. H. Tawney demonstrated in *Religion and the Rise of Capitalism*. They hated the fact that a privileged class was able to enjoy great comfort without either effort or risk, while ordinary people laboured in factories and down mines, living in constant fear of their pay being cut or their jobs lost in the event of an economic downturn.

Socialists became generically known as 'left-wing'. Yet they were, and still are, divided over how to act. Some have believed that the state should take over all capital and land, and pay people for their labour; thus the state would carry all risk, and would use all profit for the common good. Others have advocated small-scale cooperative enterprises in which the workers or the customers own the capital. Both systems have proved inefficient, and state socialism has also tended to be corrupt – although for a variety of reasons in most Western countries the state controls around 40 per cent of all economic activity.

Tawney suggested that Karl Marx, the greatest of all socialist thinkers, was in reality a direct intellectual descendant of Thomas Aquinas and the other medieval scholastics in their hatred of usury. If Marx had acknowledged his inheritance, and had thence focused more closely on how usury permeates industrial economies, his prescriptions would have been very different. Instead of urging his disciples towards bloody revolution, followed by a period in which the state controlled the economy, he would have advocated peaceful changes to the law – because by abolishing usury, society could move quite smoothly to the ends he desired.

Indeed, if socialists were to make the abolition of usury their primary goal, they would find that many of their opponents would become their partners. Just as socialism was forged in the first decades of industrialization, so too was right-wing ideology, initially called 'liberalism'. The original liberals were as opposed as the socialists to the idle upper classes secure in their wealth; if they too had considered usury, defined as the unequal allocation of risk, they would almost certainly have wanted it outlawed. Indeed, some important modern right-wing policies amount in effect to opposition to particular forms of usury.

One of the few political figures of modern times to appeal to people across the political spectrum was Mahatma Gandhi. Left-wingers identified him as a socialist who advocated local cooperation, while right-wingers saw him as a lover of personal freedom. As one of his colleagues, Babu Patwardhan, wrote in *Chalanashuddhi* (1967), the abolition of usury is the best means of achieving the kind of equitable and sustainable economy that Gandhi wanted.

6 Religion

To Jews who regard the Torah as containing the laws of God, to Christians who pay similar regard to what they consider as the first five books of the Old Testament, and to Muslims who treat the Qu'ran as the revelations of Allah, the abolition of usury is a matter of divine command. Of course, for the past four centuries or so most Jews and Christians, even those most devout in their adherence to the scriptures, have ignored the laws on usury; only Muslims have generally continued to abide by them. But ignoring religious laws does not expunge them.

There is an ancient conundrum for religious people, attributed to Socrates and known as the Euthyphro dilemma. It takes the form of a question: are particular actions good or bad because God deems them to be; or are they intrinsically good or bad, with God informing humanity of this? The first view would suggest that the usury laws, along with every other moral teaching found in the scriptures, apply only to those who accept the divine authority of the scriptures. This in turn would imply that, while Jews, Christians and Muslims should avoid usury, they should be indifferent to the actions of those outside their faiths.

In practice, in moral matters – as distinct from instructions on liturgy, diet, dress and the like – most religious people take the second view. So the scriptural verses outlawing usury should alert religious people to the probability, even the certainty, that usury is wrong. They must then work out exactly why and how it is wrong, using the kind of arguments to which any normal, decent person could give assent. And they should use the same kinds of arguments in proposing ways of reducing or eliminating usury.

Moreover, in their proposals about usury, as with all issues of public interest, religious people must be willing to compromise –

they must not let the best become the enemy of the good. In recent decades experts on Islamic finance have sought, with remarkable ingenuity, to adapt the traditional prohibition on usury to the requirements of modern finance. It is quite possible that some Christians and even Jews, once they recognize that their own faith also prohibits usury, will wish to follow the Muslim example. But it is highly unlikely within the foreseeable future that the global financial system will adopt Islamic financial practice as a whole. Instead, people of religious faith should distinguish those aspects of usury that are most harmful, and whose reduction or elimination would be most beneficial – and then seek the support of those without faith.

Yet, if a plea for a spirit of compromise seems somewhat flabby, then religious people should certainly heed the way in which God tried to persuade the Hebrew people to mend their ways: 'Let us reason the matter together' (Isaiah 1.18). Usury will only be reduced or eliminated in the modern world to the extent that reasonable people can be persuaded it is in the common interest to do so.

1

Neshek/Riba/Usury

1.1 Definition of usury

The scriptures of Judaism, Christianity and Islam are universal in their condemnation of usury. The Jewish Bible – the Old Testament – pronounces: 'You shall not lend money to my people, even to the poor amongst you; you shall not become a creditor, not shall you charge interest' (Exodus 22.25). Jesus acknowledged the existence of interest paid and charged by banks in the parable of the talents (Luke 19.23); and he condemned all lending at interest (Luke 6.35). The Qu'ran is peppered with denunciations, such as: 'Those charging usury are in the same position as those controlled by the devil's influence' (2.275).

Similar condemnations may be found in other ancient writings. In ancient Greece both Plato and Aristotle regarded usury as dishonest, while the Roman writer Cato, in *De Re Rustica*, compared usury with murder. And medieval Christian philosophers such as Thomas Aquinas, influenced by both the Bible and Aristotle, wrote at length on the evil of usurious practices.

The usual definition of usury is the lending of money at interest. But closer inspection of the scriptural texts, especially the Qu'ran, suggests that this is actually only one form. The Qu'ran observes that some people equate usury with commerce, presumably arguing that interest on loans is merely the price of money; but while 'God permits commerce, he prohibits usury' (2.275). In Arabia in Muhammad's time there was a great deal of commercial investment, particularly the financing of

11

caravans that carried goods from Mecca to Jerusalem and back; Muhammad himself was the steward of such a caravan. The Qu'ran is thus saying that investors should not lend at fixed interest to those organizing a caravan, but instead should put up their money on equal terms, sharing the risks.

The Fifth Lateran Council, convened by Pope Julius II in 1512, echoed this Qu'ranic view. It noted that money is 'a thing that produces nothing', and it defined usury as applying money 'to the acquiring of gain and profit without any work, any expense or any risk'. The Council did not outlaw investment itself, in which one person provides funds for another person for a commercial venture. Its condemnation was reserved for those situations where the investor carries no risk, and so will incur no expense if the venture fails.

Usury, then, has two elements. First, the consequences of a usurious decision must unfold over a significant period, so there is a degree of risk involved. A simple sale and purchase of a good or service can never be usurious, because the transaction is completed immediately, or at least very quickly, so there is no risk. For usury to occur, there must be a gap between the making of decisions and their results.

Second, the risk is allocated unequally, with one party having a relative degree of certainty. In the case of lending at interest for some commercial project, the lender receives the same return regardless of how the project fares; the borrower by contrast enjoys the profit if it proves successful, and carries the loss if it fails. More generally, usurious economic activities are those where one or more parties know the consequences for themselves from the outset, while at least one party does not.

This definition of usury embraces other economic acts condemned by the scriptures. The Qu'ran outlaws insurance (39.38) where an individual pays a sum in order to receive a greater sum if some adverse event occurs – thereby transferring the risk of that event to the other party. The Old Testament and Jesus Christ himself denounce in numerous places (for example

Luke 12.21) the accumulation of idle wealth as a means of protecting oneself against famine and other natural disasters; this in effect transfers the risk of such events to those without wealth, since the wealthy can protect themselves by demanding the services of the poor.

The Hadith (the sayings of Muhammad) condemn in various places – for example, in *Ash-Shifa* by Qudi Iyad – a particular kind of transaction called *gharar*. Islamic jurists have understood this as any practice involving risk, where one party carries the risk while the other party enjoys certainty. Islam traditionally distinguishes the charging of interest on loans (*riba*) from *gharar*. In fact, the crucial feature of *riba*, compared with the sharing of profits, is the unequal allocation of risk.

It will be argued later that in the modern context many loan arrangements, such as the sale of debentures by public companies, do in practice involve the sharing of risk, since in the event of default the loan contract is typically renegotiated; so such loan arrangements need not be regarded as usurious. Islamic jurists reply that the terms of a financial contract, not the outcome in the event of default, determine whether it is usurious; and it will be agreed that wise investors – of any religion or none – should follow strict Islamic practice. Nonetheless, it will be argued that, within the world of finance, the present banking system is guilty of the most acute, and most harmful, form of usury; and it is here that reform is most urgently needed.

The definition of usury proposed here also embraces acts that barely occurred in the times of Jesus and Muhammad, some of which have little impact, while others are hugely important. In addition to the financial usury of the banking system, it will be argued that there are two modern forms of usury that are especially harmful. One is taxation as it is currently levied: it is usurious through transferring a substantial portion of the 'upside' risk of enterprise and work to the state, while leaving untouched the 'downside'. The other is pollution, notably the emission of greenhouse gases: it is usurious through transfer-ring terrifying risks to future generations.

1.2 Mystery of usury

When we assess the risk or probability of some event occurring, we typically calculate the frequency with which that type of event has occurred in the past. So the actuary at an insurance company adds up the number of houses in an area that caught fire in the past year, and assesses the risk of a particular house catching fire in the coming year as that number divided by the total number of houses – setting the insurance premium accord-ingly. Similarly, in assessing the risk of a business becoming insolvent, a bank lending money sees how many similar busi-nesses have become insolvent – and sets the interest rate accord-ingly. If asked to justify this procedure, we claim that there are stable links of causation resulting in stable frequencies; some-times – as in the frequency of smokers dying of lung cancer – we can point to these links.

While not refuting this justification altogether, the scriptures of Judaism, Christianity and Islam make a serious qualification. The ultimate cause of all things, they claim, is God. And while God ordained laws governing the universe, these laws are deeply mysterious, far beyond our capacity to discern and understand (for example, Isaiah 55.8). Hence patterns and frequencies of events may change at any time in ways we cannot predict, and we have no means of assessing the probability of such a change. The story of the great flood, which appears near the start of the Jewish and Christian Bible (Genesis 7) and is repeated in the Qu'ran (7.64), is one among many scriptural stories of unexpected interruptions to the accustomed order of events.

Although he was an atheist, the philosopher David Hume shared this view. In *An Enquiry Concerning Human Understanding* (1748), he recognized that our perception of the world around us is based mainly on inductive logic, according to which we

expect the future to be similar to the past. Yet while this generally holds true, sometimes it does not; and we have no means
of predicting when inductive logic will fail. More profoundly,
our notion of causation is itself merely a matter of induction:
we claim that one type of event causes another type of event
because in the past those two types of event have always been
closely associated, with the first preceding the second. We never
actually see directly the causal links in the universe. As a result
any attempt to justify inductive logic in terms of causation is
as flawed as inductive logic itself. We are thus caught in what
became known as the 'riddle of induction': daily life requires
inductive logic, yet we cannot rely on it.

When applied to social institutions, such as an economy,
there is a deeper reason for the riddle of induction, on which
many believers and atheists would agree. If human beings
have free will, then they can act in ways that could not have
been foreseen – just as believers think God can act. Economists
mostly think that in an economy as a whole the vagaries of free
will tend to cancel themselves out, so that individuals acting
unexpectedly in one way will be offset by others acting in the
opposite way; they dignify this assumption with the name 'the
law of large numbers'. They conclude that for all practical
purposes the path of an economy is predictable, and they believe
the inaccuracies in their actual predictions arise from lack of
information. But while the law of large numbers may apply to
most natural events, there is no reason for it to apply to human
decisions. On the contrary, it is striking how the general
patterns of human behaviour change in ways that confound
even the shrewdest observers – rapid changes in fashions in
clothing being a simple example.

It follows that our assessments of risk can be no more than
informed guesses. Actuaries and bankers refer to the possibility
of interruptions in the accustomed order as 'systemic risk', and
in effect they ignore it. So if companies had been offering fire
insurance in London in early 1666, they would have had to

deafen themselves to any warnings that the entire city might burn down, because in such an event they would inevitably have failed. Similarly banks making loans prior to 2008 refused to consider the possibility that large portions of their loans might turn bad at once. Such wilful ignorance implicitly acknowledges that religion and philosophy are right.

The mysterious nature of risk also bedevils those who try to reduce or even eliminate risk through diversity. Insurance companies typically try to protect themselves against systemic risk by insuring a wide variety of different risks – sickness, death, road accidents, theft, and so on, as well as fire – or achieve the same effect through various forms of re-insurance. Similarly banks and others investing in business diversify the types of business in which they put money, in the hope that, if one type of business performs badly, others will thrive.

This strategy, however, relies as much on inductive logic as do risk calculations, and is prone to the same flaws. Any attempt to diversify risk assumes it is possible to determine which risks are independent from one another – that the risk of, say, investing in commercial property is independent from that of investing in firms making toys. Yet this is at best a matter of induction based on past experience. And there may be all sorts of links that we fail to discern: since there is a long-standing negative correlation between the birth rate and real interest rates, returns on toys and commercial property in fact may be positively correlated, albeit with a time lag. Indeed, following the crash of 2008, banks found that loans of almost every type began to turn bad simultaneously.

A modern philosopher, Nelson Goodman, has indicated a further problem with induction. In *The New Problem of Induction* (1966), he argues that our language distorts our perception of particular patterns in the world around us, and may even blind us to other patterns; since we cannot think outside our language, we have no means of knowing where our distortions and blind spots lie. Thus we may have a systematic tendency to make certain types of error in perceiving where risk exists, and no means of compensating for them. Psychologists may also point to our temperament as a factor in determining how we assess risk: so optimists tend to make low estimates of risk, while pessimists do the opposite. And the scriptures point to a further possible factor: in the Old Testament, Job's comforters exemplify a common human tendency, refuted by Job and later by Jesus (John 9.3), to regard immorality as increasing the risk of personal or economic misfortune.

So when usurers transfer risk from themselves to others, the nature of that transfer is shrouded in a double mystery. There is the mystery of risk itself, and the mystery of our perception of risk.

1.3 Inequity of usury

We normally assume that economic transactions, where the parties have entered them freely without duress – and where there is no kind of fraud – must also be equitable. When people make a purchase from a shop, or buy a block of shares in a company, we imagine that they have informed themselves as to the nature of what they are acquiring, and judge it to suit their interests. And we imagine that those making the sales have made a similar appraisal of their own interests. As a result the parties share the benefits.

Thomas Aquinas, the great medieval theologian, articulated this assumption in his theory of the just price (*Summa Theologica* 2.2). He argued that in normal circumstances transactions only occur if the sellers set the price sufficiently high for themselves to benefit, and sufficiently low for the buyers also to benefit. So marketplaces are generally moral. Half a millennium later, the great economist Adam Smith drew a similar conclusion. He observed in *The Wealth of Nations* that when we go to the baker, we are motivated by a self-interested desire for bread; he sells us bread from a self-interested desire for our money and what it can buy. So when households and bakers exchange money and bread, both achieve their purposes. And the forces of supply and demand across the market as a whole will set the price of bread at a level that reflects both the cost of producing bread and the satisfaction gained from consuming it.

However, Aquinas also explored situations where transactions become inequitable. His main example was the single supplier of a good in a particular locality, who takes advantage of a temporary shortage by pushing the price steeply upwards – such as the supplier of building materials in the wake of a natural disaster. Adam Smith went further, showing that any situation where the seller enjoys some degree of monopoly, or where all the sellers of a particular product collude to act as a monopoly, will lead to inequity. The monopolist has the power to raise the price of his goods well above their cost of production, and self-interest will prompt him to do so. So in any transaction the monopolist is liable to benefit far more than the purchaser.

When Aquinas considered usury, he effectively likened the usurer to the monopolist. In his mind the typical usurer is a money-lender taking advantage of a family that has fallen into poverty – just as the typical unjust trader is someone taking advantage of a disaster. Indeed, that is precisely the situation in which usury is condemned in the Old Testament (for example, Leviticus 25.36). Thus usury is inequitable because it favours the usurer at the expense of the other party.

But, in fact, the balance of costs and benefits in usury can never be determined – and this is the reason for its inequity. Since risk by its nature cannot be quantified, it is impossible to set a fair price for it, and hence it is impossible to include accurately the cost of risk in any transaction. As a result, if risk is allocated unequally between the parties to a transaction, it would only be pure chance if it were equitable – and only God would know if this were so. Thus we must assume that usurious arrangements are generally inequitable, albeit that we can never know the bias or the extent of the inequity. It follows that any economic arrangement involving risk can only be equitable if the risk is allocated equally between all the parties to it.

This leads to a moral paradox. Usurers may sometimes be cruel and heartless, deserving of the place allocated to them by Dante in *The Divine Comedy* (1308–21) in the inner ring of the seventh circle of hell, along with blasphemers. But equally, as Bernard Mandeville observed in *The Fable of the Bees* (1714), usurers may be motivated by thrift, putting aside money week by week in some interest-bearing asset. However, while in many contexts we regard the motive of an action as a central element of its moral worth, in the case of usury we must regard motive as irrelevant: its inequity belongs solely to the action itself, not to the state of mind of the agent. To a great degree we may resolve this paradox by recognizing that in an economy where usury is widespread, such as our own, it is virtually impossible for any individual to avoid being caught up in usurious arrangements of some kind. Hence the agent of moral change in this respect must be the laws and policies that provide the framework of individual action, rather than individuals themselves.

1.4 Paradox of usury

Adam Smith, while sharing the conviction of Thomas Aquinas that economic transactions entered into freely tend also to be fair and equitable, went far further in his analysis of how markets operate. He showed how free and fair transactions are also efficient, promoting the prosperity of society as a whole – as if by an 'invisible hand'. People's demands for different kinds of goods and services will induce entrepreneurs to start and expand firms producing them, since only by meeting demand can they make profits. This in turn will induce workers to acquire the skills needed by those firms, since in this way they can increase their wages. In addition firms will be able to enhance their profits by inventing new products and machines, thereby improving over time both the quality and the quantity of the goods and services people buy.

Adam Smith's younger contemporary David Ricardo showed in *On the Principles of Political Economy and Taxation* (1817) how the invisible hand works globally. His theory of comparative advantage demonstrates that, if countries can trade freely, each country will specialize in producing those goods for which its costs are lowest. These may be goods in which the country has some natural advantage, of which wine in Portugal was Ricardo's example; or they may be goods in which it has developed particular expertise, such as cloth in England. The result is that every country will gain.

If fair transactions are efficient, then unfair transactions must be inefficient, thwarting the invisible hand. Smith showed that this is indeed the case with monopoly and collusion between firms – and he showed that the inefficiency arises from a paradox. The monopolist raises the price for his goods by restricting the quantity he produces. On the one hand, the consequence of this restriction is that resources – labour and raw materials – are diverted to producing less desirable goods, or are wasted altogether. On the other hand, it is perfectly rational for the individual to buy those goods, so long as the price is still lower than the benefit the individual derives from the goods. So the rational behaviour of the individual is irrational for society as a whole – in the current jargon, the 'micro' and the 'macro' are at odds.

The same conflict between individual and social interests applies to usury, with far greater consequences. The moral paradox of usury is thus the mother of a series of further paradoxes that are the causes of crises not only in the economy itself, but also in social welfare and to a great extent in the environment. And while the paradoxes remain, so the crises will steadily deepen. But as with monopoly, once the paradoxes have been clarified, the way of resolving them also becomes clear – so the economy can thrive, social welfare can be secure, and, most important of all, humanity can have genuine hope of averting ecological catastrophe.

2

Tarbit/Qurud/Forms

2.1 Taxation as usury

To the ancient Hebrews land was a gift of God, to be used for his purposes (Leviticus 25.2). As a sign of this, they were required to give a tenth of the produce of their fields – the tithes – to the priests, to be used for a variety of religious and social purposes (Numbers 18.21–28). And when they harvested their fields, they had to leave a strip of corn at the edges for the poor to take (Leviticus 23.22). Islam adopted the system of tithes (*zakah*), with the Qu'ran stipulating that they should be used to feed the poor and pay their debts, ransom slaves, and look after travellers (9.60). Thus Judaism and Islam in effect imposed a tax arising from the intrinsic value of land – so that tithes and *zakah* were taxes on wealth.

When Christian kings ruled Europe, and caliphs ruled the Islamic empire, they saw themselves as appointed by God. So they continued to raise revenue mainly through taxes on land. Since agriculture dominated their economies, this revenue proved ample to finance both their armies and their palaces. But as the countries of western Europe began to industrialize, governments looked for other forms of tax. At first they taxed the money spent on the goods that the new factories produced, and then later turned their attention to the income that the owners and the workers received. By the twentieth century taxation on income and expenditure formed the great bulk of tax revenues, while many of the ancient land taxes were abolished.

John Maynard Keynes observed in 1936, in *The General Theory of Employment, Interest and Money*, that increases in tax rates beyond a certain point would reduce tax revenues. This insight received vivid expression in the late 1970s in the 'Laffer curve', named after the American economist Arthur Laffer. This shows that, if the rate of tax were either 0 per cent or 100 per cent, tax revenues would be zero; so at some rate between those two extremes tax revenue is maximized – and this marks the top of the Laffer curve. The usual explanation, offered by both Keynes and Laffer, is that, since taxes reduce the rewards for work, they must also reduce the incentive to work; and this in turn lowers the income from work that governments can tax. Economists differ over how strongly high tax rates reduce incentives, but most think that total taxes significantly above 40 per cent are likely over time to reduce the amount available to governments to spend on social welfare – so around 40 per cent is the maximum that wise governments should take in tax.

There is, however, a more profound relationship between tax rates and tax revenues, caused by the way in which taxes affect risk; and this suggests that in the long run the maximum is far lower.

The connection between tax and risk is most stark when an individual invests in a new business, or an existing firm invests in new plant and equipment – or when a firm commits itself to a lengthy programme of research and development into new products or processes. The individual or firm is risking the cost of the investment, which in a modern sophisticated economy is likely to be large. But taxation skews the risk. If the investment proves successful, the state taxes a portion of the returns; if the investment fails, the firm and its backers bear the entire loss. So taxation becomes a form of usury, with the risk of any invest-ment allocated unequally between the state and the firm: the higher the rate of tax, the more acute this asymmetry becomes.

A similar asymmetry attaches to labour also, for those people only receiving payment where they can sell the product of their work. A potter fashioning beautiful crockery, a web designer, a window cleaner, a gardener, and all the other individuals who offer their services directly to individuals and businesses, put their time at risk. Insofar as their product does not sell, or they are idle through lack of demand, they bear the entire loss. But insofar as they succeed, the state takes a portion of their income. The same applies to employees whose wage is tied to the success or failure of their employer.

So taxation on firms and on those working on their own account is a form of usury, with the risk to capital and labour allocated unequally between the state and the firm: the state enjoys a portion of the upside risk, depending on the rate of tax, while the firm or the worker carries all the downside risk. This inevitably reduces the level of investment and enterprise in an economy from what it would otherwise have been. And since investment and enterprise are the twin engines of economic growth, the effects are compounded year-on-year. If, for example, the rate of tax is such that it reduces economic growth by 1 per cent, then over five years the economy is almost 7 per cent less prosperous – and so the potential tax revenue is reduced by 7 per cent.

Although comparisons between countries are fraught with complications, this negative relationship between tax rates and growth accords with our general impression: countries with high tax rates have low growth, and hence in the long run have less to spend on social welfare. Or to put the same point another way, countries with generous welfare provision at present will have less generous welfare provision in years to come. In terms of the Laffer curve, it implies that there is not a single such curve, but a series of curves projecting into the future; and each succeeding curve has a top point at a lower rate of taxation.

2.2 Finance as usury

When money was lent at interest in the times of the Old and the New Testament, the borrower was invariably an individual or family who needed money for some private purpose, usually to alleviate poverty arising from misfortune. By the time of the Qu'ran it seems likely that rich people also lent money to finance trade, especially the caravans that went regularly from Mecca carrying goods for sale in Jerusalem – such as the caravan that the young Muhammad led.

By medieval times commercial loans had also become common in Europe, financing both trade and various productive enterprises. Thomas Aquinas recognized that such loans were quite different from private loans, in that the borrower stood to profit from them; moreover, the lender was forgoing the profit (*lucrum cessans*) he could gain from using the money for his own commercial venture. But he maintained that fixing interest on an investment made it usurious, and hence sinful; so those investing in another person's commercial venture should share the profits. Three centuries later, however, the Protestant reformer John Calvin, in *De Usuris Responsum* (1545), pronounced that the distinction between lending and sharing profits was false, in effect arguing that those making loans for commercial ventures carried the risk of the ventures failing, and hence of the borrower defaulting. So Calvin permitted loans at interest, on condition that they financed production or trade, and not consumption.

In the modern economy Calvin's argument remains valid for loans between individuals and businesses. Such lending commonly takes the form of debentures or bonds issued by companies, where companies undertake to pay those buying their bonds a fixed annual sum for a period of years, at the end of which they repay the original sum; and typically the holders of bonds are permitted to sell them to others. Where a company is in danger of insolvency, and hence likely to cease trading, its bond-holders are liable to lose much or all their investment; if such a company has a realistic hope of recovering, its bond-holders often agree to turn some or all of their bonds into shares, receiving in future a dividend dependent on profit.

So those lending directly for commercial purposes carry a degree of risk.

However, when banks act as the intermediaries between lenders and borrowers, Calvin is correct in relation to the borrowers, while Aquinas' view applies to the lenders.

When people deposit money in a bank, they are in effect lending that money to the bank; the bank pays interest, either as a monetary payment, or as a reduction in the charge for administering the money. The bank in turn lends out a large portion of that money to businesses and households, keeping only a small amount in reserve to finance withdrawals by depositors; it makes its profit from the difference between the interest it charges to borrowers and the interest it pays to depositors.

However, the allocation of risk in these two types of loan is quite different. On the one hand, depositors have the right to withdraw or transfer their deposits instantly, or after a relatively short period of notice, which is usually a few weeks and rarely longer than one or two years; and the banks make an absolute guarantee to honour that right. So the banks carry the whole of the risk, with depositors carrying none.

On the other hand, the loans made by the banks to individuals and businesses have varying terms, from a few months in the case of overdrafts to 30 years for many property loans; and they assume that some borrowers will default. They may secure the loan against some asset, which in the case of property loans is usually the property purchased with the loans, so in the event of default they can take possession of the property to repay what they are owed. But there is a danger that the value of the asset will fall below the value of the loan, while the legal process of taking possession can be slow and costly.

Thus there is an asymmetry of risk. As a result, while the loans made by banks are only partially usurious, the loans received by banks are wholly usurious.

In addition to condemning lending at interest, the Jewish, Christian and Muslim scriptures condemn in various places another financial practice, the hoarding of money and keeping it idle (for example, Matthew 6.19–21, Qu'ran 70.18). And while none of the scriptures makes a direct connection between hoarding and usury, in popular art and literature the miser and the money-lender were portrayed identically, as cold-hearted old men, alone in their heavily guarded mansions counting out their coins. This imaginative fusion contained an important insight, that the hoarding of money, holding it as an asset, is a form of lending, in which the borrower is society as a whole – and hence is a second form of financial usury.

Money represents a contract in which the holder of money can at any time require other members of society to supply goods and services of equal value. Normally people spend their money quite quickly, thus completing the contract. But when people retain money as an asset, keeping it idle, they are in effect lending to society the work or the goods that they sold for that money. And insofar as the value of money is likely to remain constant, they transfer risk to the rest of society. On the one hand, those holding money as an asset know the value of goods that their money can buy for them whenever they choose to spend it. On the other hand, the rest of society does not know the cost of supplying such goods, measured in terms of the time spent producing them: the cost may fall or rise, depending on whether the productivity of the economy rises or falls.

When Aquinas and Calvin considered matters of finance, money took the form of gold and silver, and also of paper notes issued by banks where people could deposit their gold and silver for safe-keeping – with each note representing a specific weight of silver and gold in the bank's strongroom. The value of gold and silver sometimes fluctuated in relation to the goods and services that it could buy; when European invaders brought back gold objects from the Americas in the sixteenth century and melted them down, gold fell in value, so in effect the price level rose – there was inflation. But in the long run, as Ricardo argued, the values of gold and silver reflect the labour costs of extracting them from the ground and refining them; so in relation to the cost of labour embodied in other goods, they are stable.

Today in virtually every country and society across the globe precious metals have been replaced by notes issued by a central bank which have value by government decree – hence they are called 'fiat money'. And bank deposits – accounts at banks with absolute rights of withdrawal and transfer – have replaced notes representing precious metals. The banks keep a reserve of fiat money both in their own vaults and at the central bank to finance withdrawals and transfers. But this is a small proportion of the total value of deposits; in fact the total value of bank deposits far exceeds the total amount of fiat money held by the banks and by individuals and businesses.

Typically central banks manipulate the financial markets to create a low and stable rate of inflation, usually around 2–3 per cent per year, in the conviction that this oils the wheels of commerce. So fiat money loses value by this amount. But banks are typically able to pay at least this amount of interest on 'savings accounts' requiring notice of withdrawal, while also covering their costs; indeed, the mechanisms used by central banks in creating inflation generally ensure that the interest rates on savings accounts match or exceed inflation. So money held in savings accounts maintains its value; and depositors can easily shift money savings from such accounts to current accounts with instant withdrawal.

Thus bank deposits fuse both types of financial usury. They are simultaneously loans at interest and means of holding money as an asset.

There is an added twist to the usurious nature of bank deposits. While some people may treat bank deposits as assets, everyone uses them for the normal buying and selling of goods and services. So, as the main form of money, they are the foundations of modern economies. But the nature of modern banking carries the constant risk that banks will be unable to honour their guarantee to depositors of withdrawal and transfer. If a sufficient proportion of the banks' loans turn bad, with the borrowers defaulting, their reserves of fiat money run out, and the value of their remaining loans falls below the value of their deposits; so the banks become both illiquid and insolvent. As the economic foundations start to crumble, risk now shifts from the bank to society as a whole.

2.3 Pollution as usury

There is an implicit transaction between the present generation and past and future generations. We received our economy from those who went before us, and in exchange we pass on our economy to those who come after us. Hence, if this exchange is to be equitable, we must bequeath an economy to our children and grandchildren at least as good as the economy we inherited from our parents and grandparents.

Prior to industrialization, there was no expectation that the economy would necessarily improve from one generation to the next. On the contrary, most people anticipated that their own lives would be broadly similar to those of the generation above them. And the risks attaching to the economy did not change. Certainly every generation faced the constant danger of climatic events, such as floods and droughts, that might ruin their crops; and there was always the risk of political turmoil, with potentially devastating consequences for every class of society. But so long as each generation maintained the fertility of the soil that they cultivated, and took no more wood from the forests than the forests produced, they were keeping their part of the bargain.

The advent of large-scale factories fundamentally altered the economic relationship between generations. For the first time in history human beings learnt how to make their economies grow from one decade to the next. Just as the pre-industrial economy had endured fluctuations between years of plenty and scarcity, so the industrial economies were prone to a phenomenon that became known as the 'business cycle'; and it proved as difficult to explain as the vagaries of the weather – indeed, it remains largely a enigma. But the underlying trend became an inexorably upward one, so each generation could expect to bequeath a better material standard of living than it inherited. And, since even the most mature economies, such as that of the UK – which was the first country to industrialize – have continued to grow, so the expectation of ever-greater prosperity has remained.

At the same time the industrial economies began to pass risks between the generations. When Britain created her great industrial cities, they were powered almost entirely by coal. Today, two centuries later, the new industrial countries, such as China, still rely on coal as their main source of power, albeit to generate electricity rather than to fuel giant steam engines. From the start people were aware of the damage coal soot causes to people's health, so the wealthier middle classes chose to live on the city edges or in the countryside – just as the rich in China live in shiny suburbs, far away from the power stations. Thus industrialization has always inflicted risks on the present generation.

In the last few decades, however, we have realized that much of the pollution caused by industry, and also by our patterns of consumption, is cumulative, so that each generation inflicts its pollution on its successors. Clearly the most dangerous of our pollutants are those that may contribute to the warming of the planet; and, while there are various natural processes that extract these pollutants from the atmosphere, such as the growth of trees, the rate of pollution now far exceeds the rate of extraction. So the level of pollution is rising rapidly.

While all risk is impossible to quantify, the risks associated with climate change are particularly hard to calculate. In the first place, the ecology of the planet is so complex that attempts to predict the degree of climate change, and also its effects on sea levels, fauna and flora, the incidence of floods and droughts, and so on, are little better than informed guesses. Second, while most assessments of risk depend on inductive logic by which we project the past into the future, we have no past experience of climate change caused by human activity, so we have no basis for induction. As a result, human-made climate change may prove to be a chimera. Nonetheless there is clearly a considerable danger that we shall cause the climate to change in ways that will bring great suffering to future generations; moreover, the cumulative nature of pollution implies that this risk increases from one generation to the next.

Thus pollution is a further form of usury, with the peculiarity that it spans generations. The present generation is passing to the next generation a higher level of risk than it received from the previous generation. Thus we are allocating risk away from ourselves to our children and grandchildren. Pollution is also peculiar in that, while every other form of usury involves upside as well as downside risks, the risks of pollution are almost entirely on the downside. While some, like Bjorn Lomborg (in, for example, *Cool It*, 2007), argue that global warming may bring benefits, most – even Lomborg himself – think that the costs will be far greater. So it is an extremely lopsided form of usury.

3

Dyn/Hisab/Crisis

3.1 Paradox of care

Adam Smith himself recognized that the invisible hand would not provide sufficient resources for education, so he advocated state subsidies. In the following decades various commentators, led by Jeremy Bentham, recognized the limitations of the invisible hand in the sphere of healthcare, and in providing pensions for the sick and elderly. Hence during the twentieth century governments in the developed world took over, to a greater or lesser degree, these various aspects of social welfare.

Economists today recognize three main reasons why the market mechanism falls short in the provision of social welfare. First, education and healthcare bring benefits not only to the individuals receiving them, but also to society as a whole: a well-educated and healthy workforce increases the rate of economic growth, and arguably also improves social order, to everyone's advantage. So people left to themselves will tend to spend less than is socially desirable. Second, many families are too poor to provide adequate healthcare for themselves and adequate education for their children; and education provides children, when they reach adulthood, with the opportunity to break out of poverty. Third, people cannot know in advance their needs for healthcare and pensions, while commercial forms of insurance are often very costly, and, in the case of healthcare, open to various abuses.

Moral and political philosophers, for example Michael Sandel in *Democracy's Discontents* (1996), make a fourth objection to the market mechanism in social welfare: it corrupts the relationship between providers and beneficiaries. When people buy and sell material goods to one another, the connection between buyers and sellers is largely or wholly impersonal, so self-interest is the only possible bond. But in education and healthcare the crucial connections are personal, so the quality of the relationships between teachers and their pupils, and between physicians and their patients, has a major effect on the outcomes. Thus teachers and physicians should be motivated by a degree of care and even love, as well as self-interest. It follows that, if teachers and physicians are merely selling their services to the highest bidder, the quality of education and healthcare may be compromised.

When Western governments first took on responsibility for social welfare, the costs as a proportion of total national income were comparatively modest, so they needed to raise tax rates only by a small percentage. Most children left school in their early teens and went straight to work. People mostly died soon after retirement, so their total pension was small, and their requirement for healthcare was low. Besides, the types of medical treatment available at that time were quite narrow in range and cheap to provide. But over the subsequent decades, demands have increased hugely, and so have the costs of supply.

There are two reasons for this increased demand. The first is longevity: even since as recently as 1950, life expectancy in most mature economies has risen by almost two decades. So the period of drawing a pension has multiplied, as have the requirements of the elderly for healthcare. The second, more fundamental reason is higher incomes. As people have grown richer, so their desire for material goods – electrical goods, clothes, food – has largely been satisfied; and, besides, as manufacturing industry has become more automated, the price of most material goods has fallen sharply. As a result people increasingly demand services that improve the quality of their own and their children's lives – especially better education and healthcare. In addition, they want to ensure that their old age will be comfortable. In the language of economics, social welfare has very high 'income elasticity of demand'.

There are also two reasons for the increased cost of supply. The first is that medical advances have hugely widened the range of treatments for various illnesses, and the costs of these treatments are often high. The second, more fundamental reason is that education and healthcare are generally very labour intensive, with limited scope for automation. Indeed, the best methods of education today are little different from those used in Plato's Academy in ancient Athens, while nurses in our hospitals perform the same types of task as Florence Nightingale specified. As a result, while the costs of manufactured goods have been dropping, the costs of social welfare have been rising.

The consequence is that in mature Western economies governments find themselves caught in a paradox – the paradox of care. On the one hand, people want their governments to meet their ever-higher demands for social welfare and they are highly critical of governments that fail to do so. On the other hand, they resist paying the ever-higher taxes required to supply those demands. And even if they were willing, the usurious nature of taxation – as we have seen – would thwart their intentions, with higher tax rates reducing in the long run the revenues from taxation. So for governments to impose higher taxes in order to bring about the improvement of social welfare would be self-defeating.

This paradox is made more acute by the progressive nature of most taxation. Governments seek to use taxation as a means of reducing inequalities of income. They levy higher rates of tax on higher levels of income, and also impose taxes on wealth, such as the gains made on the sale of shares and other assets. There is thus a rising 'marginal rate of tax'. Yet when entrepreneurs consider starting or expanding businesses, it is the marginal rate of tax that they consider, since this defines the proportion of any prospective returns that the state will take. So progressive taxation reduces the rewards for risk still further, discouraging entrepreneurs from taking risks – and depressing still further the revenues from tax needed to pay for social welfare.

In fact, the desire to reduce inequalities gives an extra twist to the paradox of care. If governments simply provided or subsidized education and healthcare for the poor, while requiring the majority of people to pay for themselves, social welfare expenditure would itself promote equality. Moreover, the tax revenues needed to pay for it would be far smaller, reducing the usurious effects of taxation. Instead, governments typically provide or subsidize education and healthcare in virtually equal measure for everyone, with little consequent effect on relative incomes. So progressive taxation becomes their main weapon against inequality. And, since the tax revenues required for universal social welfare are so large, the usurious effects of taxation are even greater.

The effect of the paradox of care is to render social welfare chronically short of funds. If expenditure on social welfare reflected both the direct benefits to the recipients and the wider benefits to society as a whole, it would be far higher. Indeed, for most people expenditure on their own welfare is far lower than would be the case if, instead of paying through taxation, they paid for themselves. And in the coming decades the paradox is set to become even more acute in many countries, as the decline in both the birth rate and the death rate pushes up the proportion of the population that requires pensions and also needs treatment for chronic illnesses.

3.2 Paradox of thrift

In 1714 Bernard Mandeville, a Dutchman who settled in England, published a satire on thrift. In *The Fable of the Bees* he depicted a beehive whose inhabitants are dedicated to material pleasure, and hence eager to acquire the goods that yield pleasure. Thus the hive is wealthy and hard-working, with the bees demanding from one another as much as they can produce. But the bees feel guilty about their materialism, regarding it as sinful. Suddenly this guilt becomes unbearable and they convert to virtue, becoming frugal in their consumption. Hence they save most of their income, hoarding most of the money that they earn. As a result their demand for each other's work plummets, condemning the hive to perpetual poverty and idleness – reflecting the idleness of their money. Mandeville concluded that 'private vice' brings 'public benefits', and, more importantly, private virtue brings public costs – the paradox of thrift.

Since Mandeville's *Fable* provoked widespread shock, especially among people of religious convictions, it seems likely that Thomas Malthus was aware of it. But for him thrift was a matter not of moral virtue, but of rational calculation. Moreover, he distinguished two forms of thrift, one involving risk and the other avoiding it. Risky thrift was typified in Malthus' mind by the factory owner ploughing a portion of his profits back into his business, expanding his factory and buying more machinery. Yet there was always the possibility that market conditions might turn against him. Hence the wise factory owner also engaged in safe thrift, setting aside a portion of his profits in forms that retained their value. One form was agricultural land, so Malthus was not surprised that factory owners frequently purchased country estates. But the easiest form was money; so each week, in Malthus' mind's eye, the factory owner placed a leather pouch of coins in the safe in the basement of his villa, or else took it to a local banker whom he could trust.

Malthus believed that safe thrift, especially the accumulation of gold and silver, represented a constant drain on total demand, dragging the economy downwards into chronic depression – and leaving a large portion of the workforce unable to find work.

John Maynard Keynes, who was well read in the history of economic thought, was aware of both Mandeville's *Fable* and Malthus' theory of thrift. He believed it was no longer just wealthy businessmen who practised thrift, but also families in almost every class of society. In Britain and other industrialized nations wages and salaries had risen sharply since the late nineteenth century, so the majority of people no longer had to spend their entire income on survival. As a result they were able to save money each week to pay for healthcare when they fell ill, to help educate their children and grandchildren, and to provide a pension in old age.

Keynes recognized that current 'dis-saving' by families on healthcare and education, and by old people spending their pensions, would partly offset saving by other families for future needs. But people will always wish to accumulate a bigger stock of wealth than they anticipate needing, partly to protect themselves from unexpected misfortunes – 'saving for a rainy day' – and partly as a legacy to the next generation. Keynes acknowledged the ability of governments to blunt the desire to save by providing social welfare – which in the 1930s the British government already did, to a limited extent. But the usurious nature of taxation imposes such constraints on governments' expenditure that they can never satisfy people's demands.

Keynes' main insights were into the mechanisms of thrift within the economy of his time. Initially thrifty families would look for safe financial assets that yielded an income. So, either directly or through some kind of fund, they would buy bonds in large well-established companies. This would push down the interest rates payable on bonds, encouraging companies to issue new bonds for investment in plant and machinery. But the more that households saved, the less they spent on the goods that companies produced. So typically the total savings by households would exceed the amount that companies wished to invest. As a result households would purchase existing bonds, as well as new bonds, pulling up their price, and hence pushing down their yield – the annual payments as a proportion of price.

At the same time, the shortfall in total demand would hold down the prices that firms were able to charge for their goods and services, so inflation would fall virtually to zero, or even to below zero. Hence money would now hold its value. As a result, as the yields on bonds fell, people would be increasingly willing to hold money – either fiat money or bank deposits – as an alternative. Eventually all additional savings would take the form of money – a situation which Keynes described as the 'liquidity trap'.

Keynes believed that the economy would always move up and down in cycles. In particular, as the economy moved downwards, households would severely reduce their savings in order to maintain their normal consumption. So the economy would never be permanently caught in the liquidity trap. But, like Malthus, he argued that there was a chronic tendency for savings to exceed investment, and hence a chronic bias towards high unemployment. Ultimately the excess savings took the form of households hoarding money, holding it idle as an asset. So, although neither Keynes nor Malthus used the term in this context, they both regarded usury as the source of the paradox of thrift.

Later followers of Keynes, such as Hyman Minsky in *The Financial Instability Hypothesis* (1978), have extended his analysis, emphasizing the role of banks as repositories of excess savings. As thrifty households pour their savings into the banks, the banks look for safe ways to lend this incoming money. They soon run out of reliable businesses wanting money, and instead they start offering larger loans for people to buy assets that appear safe – especially property, since it is both tangible and can act as its own security for loans. Moreover, as the glut of savings forces down interest rates, people can afford larger loans. In some small degree this might stimulate the construction of more property; but it will mainly push up the price of existing property.

As property owners become wealthier, more and more people want to buy a larger house than they need, and to buy a second home. Moreover, they come to regard their property as a form of savings – 'my home is my pension' – so they reduce their normal savings and increase their consumption. Thus the property market fuels an economic boom. But it has also become a vast Ponzi scheme: just as in a classic Ponzi scheme the fraudster pays returns from money newly invested, so in the housing market rising values depend on ever larger amounts being lent to those buying property. Eventually the banks run out of excess savings, causing the property market to collapse and the economy to slump. The banks themselves totter into insolvency, threatening a sudden collapse in the quantity of money in circulation – and thence threatening a sudden contraction in normal economic transactions, as occurred in the USA after the Wall Street crash of 1929.

Thus for Minsky it is not simply the hoarding of money, but the double form of usury practised by banks, that is the source of the paradox of thrift.

In the popular mind Keynes and his followers are associated with 'fiscal stimuli', in which the government resolves the paradox of thrift by spending more than it raises in taxation. In fact, while Keynes argued that fiscal stimuli could be effective in the short run, he believed they could not be sustained. The key problem is financing the difference between spending and taxation – the fiscal deficit. One possibility is for the government to borrow money, issuing bonds. But if this continues, the rising amount of interest payments will push the government towards insolvency; as potential lenders anticipate this, they will stop lending. The other possibility is to print money. But this will create an ever larger stock of money; as the money finds its way into the banks, it will fuel an even greater surge in property prices and boom in consumption, to be followed by an even greater slump. Thus Keynes offered no permanent solution to the paradox of thrift.

Even as Keynes' great work, known to economists simply as *The General Theory*, was first appearing in bookshops, the march of events seemed to be resolving the paradox of thrift. By 1936 German rearmament was beginning to stimulate the European economies, and as Britain began to boost its military spending in response, unemployment fell rapidly. Then, after the outbreak of the Second World War, Keynes found himself advising the British government how to avoid inflation. Within a year of the end of the war, Keynes was dead. Governments, however, had no choice but to finance the massive task of reconstruction through spending far more than they raised in taxation, creating a shortage of labour; even when the bomb-sites had all been cleared, they continued to try and please their voters by keeping taxes lower than spending. Thus by the 1960s even economists, let alone politicians, had come to imagine that Keynes had advocated persistent fiscal deficits – which were now called 'Keynesian policies'.

But far from resolving the paradox of thrift, Keynesian policies in fact gave it a new twist – the twist that Keynes feared might occur during the war. By maintaining high total demand, fiscal deficits pulled up wages and prices; and, as workers anticipated further increases in prices, they demanded even higher wages to compensate. Thus in the 1970s Western economies became caught in a spiral of accelerating inflation – which in many cases rose to over 25 per cent a year. Governments now escaped the consequences of their past profligacy, since inflation eroded the value of the debts they had incurred. But the victims were those who held those debts: governments by means of inflation were in effect stealing from their creditors.

Inevitably, as the public in Western countries awoke to what was occurring, they reacted with disgust, demanding that their governments control inflation. So in the 1980s most governments abandoned Keynesian policies. Quite unjustly, Keynes himself was discredited in many eyes.

But now many countries in Asia were developing rapidly, while their people saved a very high proportion of their incomes to pay for healthcare, education and pensions. At the same time the banking system had become global. Excess Asian savings soon found their way into Western banks, creating the greatest surge in property prices and longest consumption boom in history – followed in 2007/08 by the worst financial and economic crisis at least since Keynes was in his prime.

Thus the paradox of thrift has become a global phenomenon.

3.3 Paradox of greenness

In 1972 the Club of Rome, an international think-tank, published a report, *The Limits to Growth*, on the relationship between the economy and ecology, crystallizing concerns that a number of commentators had already been expressing. The report argued that natural resources, including fossil fuels, were rapidly being depleted, while various forms of pollution caused by their use were accumulating. It concluded that, unless humanity found ways of drastically reducing its dependence on fossil fuels and other resources, it would face both economic and ecological catastrophe.

During the subsequent decades scientists have come to focus on global warming as the greatest ecological danger, and hence on greenhouse gas emissions as the most dangerous type of pollution. As these emissions are caused mainly by the production of energy, there has been extensive discussion about alternative forms of energy that are ecologically sustainable. Now even small children are aware of how sunlight and wind, waves and tides might be harnessed. Moreover, since these sources of energy are abundant and free, it seems likely that human ingenuity may find ways of harnessing them more cheaply than pumping oil or digging coal from the ground and burning it; so 'green' energy could bring direct economic, as well as environmental, benefits.

Yet remarkably little human ingenuity has actually been devoted to this task – far, far less than to exploring new sources of oil, or even to developing new forms of financial usury. The various green energy technologies currently available remain crude and expensive, dependent on large subsidies from taxpayers or consumers.

The reason for this failure is that the development of green energy technologies is highly risky, so it has been starved of funds. Developing new technologies of any kind is inherently uncertain, because during the period of development there are no returns, and at the end the technology may fail. But the development of green energy technologies is especially risky. Whereas most new technologies are aimed at creating a new product, the primary purpose of green energy technologies is to produce an existing product, namely electricity, in a different manner. So there is a dual standard of success: as well as being much cleaner than fossil fuels, they must also be cheaper.

The shortage of funds is made more acute by the usury of finance and taxation. The global glut of savings implies there is ample money to invest in green energy technologies. But households saving for the future want to know their money is safe, and so in large measure deposit in banks; in order to honour their guarantees, banks too want a high level of security, plus immediate returns to cover their costs and pay interest. So, although for many people the prospect of global warming evokes the most profound anxiety, very few are willing to put their money into assuaging this anxiety. Some justify their reluctance by asserting that it is the duty of governments to subsidize investment in green energy technologies, so governments should raise taxes to provide such subsidies. But, by reducing the potential rewards for private investors, higher tax rates would merely make the shortage of funds even more acute.

Although it may be politically inexpedient to say so, it is surely green energy's poor record that deters governments from taking harsher measures against greenhouse gas emissions. There have been rare instances where governments have banned other pollutants, confident that firms would soon discover clean alternatives that were no more expensive. For example, following the discovery that CFCs from refrigerators and aerosols were destroying the ozone layer, 40 governments in 1987 signed the Montreal Protocol, requiring that their use be halved by 1999; in the event, anxious to preserve their markets, the manufacturers found substitute chemicals in ample time. But when it comes to the major challenge on which our planet's future may depend, that of replacing fossil fuels in electricity generation and transport, governments look at the feeble record of research, and draw back – fearful that announcing a ban on fossil fuels within 10 or 20 years would provoke economic collapse.

In the face of the appalling threat of global warming, it is tempting to imagine that governments should simply take control of their economies. Indeed, it has become fashionable to urge governments to tackle the environmental crisis by the same political means that they adopted in the two world wars, allocating labour and capital as required. So governments would determine how many people worked in education and healthcare, and how many devoted themselves to technological research. Unfortunately, seven decades of communism taught us that such central government control, while it may be effective in an immediate national emergency, soon sinks into a bog of inefficiency, corruption and tyranny. In fact, communism has shown itself to cause far more pollution than the invisible hand.

Thus humanity is caught in a paradox of greenness, which is ultimately far more serious than the paradoxes of care and thrift. Across the world there is agreement that drastically reducing greenhouse gas emissions is the single most important challenge over the coming decades, the potential cost of failure being the decimation of the human population and the extinction of innumerable other species. Moreover, there is widespread belief in our ability to develop the necessary technology, so that we can meet the challenge without seriously damaging our material living standards. Yet as individuals we turn away from the opportunities to realize that belief. We may be willing to install energy-saving devices in our homes, to drive cars that use less fuel, and to forgo air travel that we deem unnecessary. But in our hearts we know these are little more than gestures. And we are not willing to invest our savings in developing technologies that might genuinely help to save our planet from catastrophe.

4

Zedek/Mudaraba/Equity

4.1 Just welfare

To resolve the paradox of thrift, we must first resolve the paradox of care. Providing for future welfare is the main motive for thrift, and it would be utterly wrong to discourage thrift unless there were other means of providing welfare. So just forms of welfare are the foundations of just economics.

The limitations of market mechanisms in the provision of social welfare, and the moral objections to such market mechanisms, suggest five essential requirements for just welfare. First, it must provide a good standard of social welfare to all people regardless of income. Second, in order to reduce the usurious effects of taxation, people must finance welfare directly rather than through the government. Third, it must not depend on savings, so current contributions should finance current expenditure. Fourth, expenditure should reflect the relative importance that people attach to social welfare; so, as the economy grows, social welfare should grow faster. And fifth, it should foster, within the spheres of education and healthcare, benevolent personal relationships between providers and beneficiaries.

In the past the extended family was the primary source of social welfare, and it fulfilled all five criteria for just welfare. In the first place, the extended family looked after all its members, regardless of their economic value. It was largely self-sufficient, taking pride in what it could do for itself. And at any moment the adults enjoying good health looked after the young, the sick and the elderly. In effect, therefore, the extended family acted as a kind of insurance in which the premiums took the form, not of money, but of labour. In addition, relationships within the family, while they sometimes become hateful, display in general the greatest benevolence. So the extended family – writ large – should be the model for a modern system of social welfare.

Many centuries ago English law invented a structure that replicates this aspect of family life, namely the trust. Just as the healthy members of the extended family used part of their time for the benefit of all the members, so trustees have charge of particular assets and resources on behalf of the trust's beneficiaries. Social welfare, then, should take the form of a series of trusts, to which people make financial contributions year-on-year, and from which they receive welfare as and when they need it.

In the first instance – and perhaps permanently – the social trusts would be national or regional; they might be run as arms of government, or as autonomous bodies regulated by the state. There would be a separate trust for each aspect of social welfare, so one trust would devote itself to education, another to healthcare, and so on. The main difference between national social trusts and present forms of social welfare would be the method of funding. Instead of receiving money from the pool of taxation, the national social trusts would receive a direct contribution from each household, similar to the direct contribution paid by households in the UK to the BBC; everyone would have to pay a basic contribution to each trust. In addition households could choose to pay more for improved services, such as a private room in hospital or a higher pension in old age. As the economy grew, so the level of contributions would tend to rise even faster.

Once national social trusts had been established, it would then be feasible for voluntary social trusts to spring up, allowing people to opt out of the national social trusts. There would then be healthy competition between trusts. Some voluntary trusts might be based on a common religious or ethical outlook, others might be rooted in a particular locality, and so on. Some voluntary trusts might run their own services: so a healthcare trust might decide to run its own surgeries and hospitals, and an educational trust might run its own schools, with members having free access as required. Other voluntary trusts might simply act as a conduit for funds, with members spending on schools, hospitals and so on that were run independently. And some voluntary trusts might invite people to contribute in part through their work, giving their time and skills in exchange for a lower payment – an arrangement that might especially suit older people. The voluntary social trusts would be subject to the same regulations as the national social trusts, with the state having inspectors to enforce the regulations; and the minimum levels of contribution would be the same.

There is a profound difference between a trust and a normal company: while the directors of a company have a duty to maximize the profits of the shareholders, the duty of trustees is to maximize the well-being of the beneficiaries. There are numerous examples across the world, including in many poor areas of Africa and Asia, of companies running excellent schools and hospitals; so where a social trust or its members are purchasing education and healthcare from external providers, they should have no inhibition in dealing with companies. But the social trusts themselves should retain the legal structure and the ethos of a trust. In the case of a voluntary social trust, the beneficiaries should elect the trustees. More importantly, where a trust has failed them, individual beneficiaries should have the right to act against the trustees for breach of trust.

A system of social welfare trusts, whether national or voluntary, would be subject to risk, since the current level of provision would depend on the current level of contributions. And the government would have the continuing responsibility of setting the current basic contribution, balancing the needs of those having to pay the contribution with the needs of those receiving benefits. In the coming decades, as the populations of most countries grow older, this balance will become increasingly hard to strike. But the risk would be fair, allocated equally across the population – just as risks borne by families are fair.

The creation of social trusts, and the transfer of other state functions to the private sector, would hugely reduce the tax revenues that governments would require. To decrease taxation further governments should, wherever feasible, confine their expenditure to those services that they alone can perform, of which the enforcing of the law and national defence are central, and make other services, such as the provision of trunk roads, dependent on direct contributions by users.

Yet the state would need to subsidize the contributions to social trusts of those too poor to pay them, and also to provide such social welfare as the trusts failed to cover, including payments to the disabled and the unemployed. Indeed, apart from preserving order, the main purpose of taxation would be to redistribute finance from rich to poor – to act as a modern Robin Hood. And since overall public spending would be much lower, the state could afford to be generous in its subsidies to the poor, provided it did not unduly blunt the incentives for them to lift themselves out of poverty.

To minimize the usurious effects of such tax as was still raised, governments should concentrate on those forms of taxation that impose the least penalties on effort and risk. Indirect taxes levied on expenditure are undoubtedly better than direct taxes on income and profits, since those taking risks can avoid such taxes if they plough back their income into their businesses. Better still, the government should tax wealth that its holders have done nothing to create. In 1879 an American economist, Henry George (in *Progress and Poverty*), urged governments to eliminate poverty by imposing an annual levy on the 'unim-proved value' of land, which in effect would be a revival of the main ancient form of taxation. His proposal has subsequently gained a long line of supporters on all sides of the political spectrum, from the great right-wing economist Milton Friedman to many socialists and environmentalists; many Islamic jurists have also indicated approval. It is doubtful whether in the modern context such a levy would be sufficient. But the underlying point is that charges on unearned wealth are the only form of taxation totally untainted by usury, and hence should be the primary means of raising revenue.

4.2 Just economics

While just welfare would greatly reduce people's desire for risk-free savings, many would still want a sum of money to top up the trusts' provisions, and to provide a legacy for their children and grandchildren. As the economy grew, making them richer, they would continue to put an ever greater premium on such financial security. So, while resolving the paradox of care would eliminate the necessity for thrift, it would not eliminate thrift itself. Hence the paradox of thrift must be resolved directly.

Moreover, resolving the paradox of thrift is essential for resolving the paradox of greenness. While people can hold their money idly and be certain that it will retain its value, they will never take the necessary risks of investing in the development of green technology.

Since the financial usury practised by the banks is the main source of the paradox of thrift within modern economies, the paradox can only be resolved by transforming the banking system to make such usury impossible. This can be achieved by two simple measures. First, the government and central bank should declare that they are no longer guaranteeing bank deposits, and will thus provide no help to banks that become insolvent. Second, the central bank should only license banks to accept deposits if they take no risks whatever. The effect of these two measures would be to split the banking system in two: there would be deposit banks – sometimes known as narrow banks – administering their depositors' money; and separately there would be 'capital banks'. The same parent company might own both a deposit and a capital bank, but there would be a strict separation of their funding.

When a deposit bank received fiat money, it would send a proportion to the central bank to finance transfers between depositors at different banks, while placing the rest in its vaults. It would then be allowed to spend a proportion from its vaults on government bonds and short-term government bills, which are completely safe. But this latter proportion should not be so high as to threaten a bank's ability to finance withdrawals and transfers on demand. Nor should it be so high as to enable the deposit banks to pay a significant premium to depositors. On the contrary, the limit should be set so that the costs incurred by the deposit banks in administering people's deposits should generally be approximately the same as the income they receive from government bonds and bills.

Thus money in the form of bank deposits would depreciate by approximately the rate of inflation – just as fiat money depreciates at exactly the rate of inflation. So people would no longer hold money as an asset.

Capital banks by contrast would use the money invested with them to provide finance to businesses and households, much in the way that present banks do. But, in the absence of any government guarantee, they could no longer promise the amount that depositors could withdraw or the timing of withdrawals; indeed, any such promise would be fraudulent. Instead, they would pay their depositors each year a premium depending on the returns they received on their loans and other forms of finance, less the losses they incurred from borrowers defaulting; if the losses exceeded the returns, this premium would turn into a charge. While they would be required to keep a reserve of fiat money to pay depositors wishing to withdraw, they would have the right to limit or even stop withdrawals in the event of their reserve becoming depleted.

Capital banks would thus simply provide another channel for people to invest their money indirectly, alongside mutual funds and investment companies; potential depositors would choose those whose investment policies appealed to them, and whose managers seemed shrewd in implementing those policies. Some capital banks might choose not to make loans to firms and households, but instead acquire some kind of ownership of the assets for which they provide finance. For example, in helping families to acquire a house, they would have a stake in the value of the house, and families would pay a rent for that stake. In recent years Islamic banks have developed a range of financial arrangements of this kind to replace the various forms of loans that secular banks currently make, and these frequently prove highly satisfactory both to the recipients and to the banks themselves. But whether or not to imitate Islamic banking should be a matter of choice for capital banks and their depositors, not a subject of legislation.

The central bank would continue to cause inflation. This should be sufficiently high to discourage people from holding money as an asset, but not so high as to disrupt normal transactions: the current target shared by most central bankers of 2–3 per cent a year is probably right. The central bank would now have much more powerful means of hitting its inflation target. At present central banks try to adjust total demand in the economy by manipulating short-term interest rates. Instead, they could affect total demand directly by altering the quantity of fiat money in circulation, which in turn would directly affect total deposits at deposit banks. Since people would only hold money for transactions, and not as an asset, the velocity of money circulating in the economy would be stable; so changing the quantity of fiat money would have a proportionate effect on the amount spent. The method of altering the quantity of fiat money would be the buying and selling of government bonds in exchange for fiat money.

Governments should commit themselves to gradually repaying the bulk of their accumulated debt, thereby reducing the total amount of government bonds. This would eliminate the possibility of people holding government bonds as a substitute for money. It would also lift from future generations the burden of paying interest on that debt, which is itself a form of usury. Yet the creation of social welfare trusts would allow governments to achieve this without running a fiscal surplus, taxing more than they spend. Instead governments would gradually sell their social welfare assets – hospitals, schools, and so on – to the social welfare trusts, which would buy them from the contributions they received. Thus it would be higher contributions to social welfare trusts, rather than higher taxes, that would repay existing government debt.

There would still, however, be cyclical movements in the economy, and there would still be emergencies – natural disasters and perhaps wars – requiring governments to increase their spending at short notice. So governments would still at times need to spend more than their tax revenues, and hence issue new bonds. But governments could increase taxes at the top of the cycles to buy back their bonds, so their debt would not accumulate.

People would now only be able to accumulate wealth by making investments in which they shared risk. And the projected rates of return would ensure equality between the finance that people wished to supply and the finance that firms demanded for plant, machinery, and so on. If people were supplying too much finance, firms would be able to offer a lower pro-jected return – they could issue shares or debentures at a higher price. This would induce them to demand more and people to supply less finance, until supply and demand were the same.

There is an important added advantage to the division of the banks and the withdrawal by government of its guarantee. By guaranteeing bank deposits the government also in effect guarantees the survival of existing banks, regardless of how inefficiently they are managed. In most countries the banks are notoriously inefficient, with a few large, well-established banks offering a similarly low quality of service at a high cost. So banks are uniquely insulated from the gales of 'creative destruction', which, according to Joseph Schumpeter in *Capitalism, Socialism and Democracy* (1942), are essential for maintaining economic vigour. Once the banks were divided, it would be relatively easy for new deposit and capital banks to rise up, offering a better service at a lower cost – so the gales would blow.

It is unlikely that every major country would adopt such policies simultaneously. So a particular country adopting them might still be the recipient of excess savings from other countries. This danger would be partly offset by the capital banks no longer guaranteeing the value of the money invested with them or the right of withdrawal. Nonetheless capital banks specializing in finance for property might still prove attractive when the property market was stable or rising, since such finance is secured against the property; and this might provoke a further surge in property prices.

While any subsequent collapse in property prices would no longer endanger normal economic transactions – since these would be conducted through deposit banks – the overall volatility of property prices would accentuate the normal cycles in total demand. In the first place, as in the past, rising property prices might induce a temporary boom in consumption. More importantly, the excess savings poured into the country would push its exchange rates upwards, reducing demand for its exports; when property prices collapsed, the exchange rate would fall, causing a sudden increase in export demand. So the rise in the property market would be mirrored by a trade deficit, which would be corrected as the property market fell. And in the process businesses exporting a large proportion of their goods would suffer severe disruption.

During the Bretton Woods negotiations in 1944, when the Allied countries formed the rules and institutions that would govern international trade after the Second World War, John Maynard Keynes anticipated the problem of countries exporting their excess savings, and thereby enjoying a trade surplus while pushing other countries into deficit. He proposed that countries with trade surpluses should be fined, so they would have to implement policies to reduce their savings and increase their own total demand. Unfortunately the USA, which then had a large trade surplus and was exporting surplus savings, rejected Keynes' proposal. But even if Keynes' proposal had been adopted, it would not have worked, since in the long run, under the present system of banking, governments are powerless to eliminate excess savings.

Thus countries adopting just money and investment should be willing to impose a tariff on imports in order to protect themselves from excess savings. The fairest tariff would be that advocated by the Cambridge Economic Policy Group in the 1970s, taking the form of a flat percentage of the value of imports, imposed on all foreign goods and services indiscriminately – and adjusted annually to keep imports in balance with exports.

There is a widespread fear of tariffs and other forms of trade protection among policy-makers and economists. They assume that, if one country imposes a tariff, other countries will retaliate by imposing a tariff on that country's exports to them. It is also commonly believed that trade protection, by reducing world trade, greatly worsened the depression of the 1930s. The Cambridge Economic Policy Group argued that a general tariff, imposed with the sole intention of maintaining total demand, would be less likely to provoke retaliation than specific tariffs to protect particular industries.

Yet even in the event of retaliation, the effects would be quite different from those experienced 80 years ago. In recent decades the typical scale of production has fallen dramatically, thanks to new technology and the shift to services. So firms can flourish, and competition can be maintained, in much smaller markets. And most services currently traded can be produced locally with little loss of efficiency. Moreover, a reduction in the volume of goods transported across the world by air, ship and truck would significantly reduce carbon emissions.

4.3 Just ecology

By increasing the proportion of income spent on healthcare and education, and thence reducing the proportion of expenditure on manufactured goods, just welfare would cause an immediate reduction in greenhouse gas emissions. Teaching the young and treating the sick use tiny amounts of energy compared with operating factories and transporting their output across the world.

Much more important, however, is the effect that just economics would have on the funds available for developing green energy technologies. People wishing to accumulate wealth would have to find productive businesses in which to invest, either directly in their own name, or indirectly through capital banks, mutual funds and so on. And the reduction or elimination of usurious forms of taxation would increase people's appetite for risk. While investors would be likely to allocate some of their money to large well-established companies that they regarded as relatively safe, many would also recognize that smaller companies with imaginative plans for the future often offer better long-term returns – including companies developing green energy technologies.

So for the first time such companies would have access to ample funds. This would create a double opportunity. On one hand, governments could afford to be bold in introducing tough sanctions against greenhouse gases, knowing that firms might at last find clean methods of generating green energy able to compete with fossil fuels. On the other hand, tough sanctions against greenhouse gases would greatly increase the prospective returns on green energy technology, since the demand for it would shoot upwards. As a result government would replicate the virtuous circle that eliminated CFCs in the 1990s without any reduction of living standards.

The question, then, is what form the sanctions on greenhouse gases should take.

When economists such as A. C. Pigou (in *The Economics of Welfare*, 1920), first began to consider the control of pollution, they generally advocated taxation. The government, they proposed, should measure the cost of pollution to society as a whole, and then impose a tax equal to that cost. With those forms of pollution whose effects are mainly confined to their immediate victims, such as noise and soot, economists have developed reasonably reliable means of estimating costs; for example, the cost of airport noise is reflected in the decline of house prices and rents in the vicinity. But where the pollution accumulates, threatening future generations more than the present one, any calculation will be little more than an informed guess. In 2006 *The Stern Report* made a brave attempt at putting numbers to the costs and risks to future generations of our emissions of greenhouse gases; but only three years later Nicholas Stern was declaring that his estimates were seriously awry, and should be revised upwards (*New Scientist*, 21 January 2009).

A much-touted alternative to pollution taxes is pollution trading, and there have been several attempts to establish structures for trading in emissions of carbon dioxide, the main greenhouse gas. The idea is that governments set each year a maximum total quantity of carbon emissions, and either distribute or auction carbon permits equal to this total. Holders of these permits can then trade them. So, for example, electricity companies installing low-carbon methods of generation can recoup part of the costs by selling their permits to companies making no efforts to restrain their emissions. In subsequent years governments gradually reduce the quantity of carbon permits, putting increasing pressure on companies to find means of reducing pollution. This in turn encourages other companies engaged in developing green technology to accelerate their efforts, knowing that they will have a market for their products.

While in principle carbon trading should be effective, in practice it has four major drawbacks. First, determining the total quantity of carbon permits is susceptible to political pressure by the major polluters; this has proved especially damaging to the Emissions Trading Scheme instituted by the European Union. Second, it is difficult to measure and monitor the actual amount of carbon emitted by any particular company. Third, the price of carbon permits is liable to fluctuate, making it difficult for companies to determine the returns on installing technologies to reduce pollution. Fourth, without some elaborate system of 'smart cards', carbon trading cannot apply to households and small businesses, but is confined to large-scale polluters, such as those producing electricity, cement, steel and so on. As a result of these drawbacks the initial enthusiasm for carbon trading is waning.

There is also a moral objection to carbon trading. The usurious nature of pollution, in which we impose incalculable risks on future generations, implies that every corporation and country has a moral obligation to reduce carbon emissions. If some corporations and countries can in effect pay others to reduce emissions on their behalf, they are using their wealth to evade that obligation.

Since the risks posed by climate change are so huge, and since they appear to be increasing rapidly year-on-year, the only realistic hope of mitigating these risks is to eliminate altogether the main sources of greenhouse gases. The only means of achieving this is the force of law, the banning of those sources – which accords with the primary purpose of law, to prevent people from doing harm to others. Thus governments should declare that by a certain date, perhaps 10 or 15 years hence, households and businesses will no longer be permitted to use fossil fuels, or substitutes with similar effects.

This announcement would immediately cause the virtuous circle of investment to start spinning. Anticipating that, as the date approached, the demand for green energy technology would rise rapidly, investors would be eager to provide funds for any firm that might help to meet this demand. So the pace of development would rapidly accelerate.

Dealing with climate change through taxes and carbon trading has been further hindered by the need for international agreement: since taxes and trading impose higher costs on firms subject to them, countries fear that, if they were to act alone, their export costs would rise, and so their industries would suffer. In the case of an outright ban on fossil fuels, the opposite would almost undoubtedly apply. Individual countries announcing a ban would give a huge boost to the manufacture and installation of green technology by their own companies, and hence enjoy the advantages of being the 'first movers'. Moreover, if, as seems likely, green energy generated on a large scale were to prove cheaper than that generated using fossil fuels, the pioneering countries would find themselves selling and installing green energy technologies across the world – so their exports would rise.

Most countries today have laws of various kinds covering in minute detail almost every aspect of life. Although the intentions of these laws are usually benign, they often have harmful consequences that were not anticipated. So an outright ban on fossil fuels should be combined with a rigorous review of all other laws that may hinder households and businesses from saving energy or using green energy. The most important such laws are those on the use of land and buildings. There is undoubtedly huge scope for houses and commercial buildings to generate green energy, as well as for their energy consumption to be reduced; and the law must allow experiment and innovation, even if the initial results are sometimes unsightly. New forms of energy and energy-saving may also have implications for our patterns of settlement, perhaps favouring larger back yards and gardens; here too the law should be permissive, rather than restrictive. The law should also allow and encourage whatever new forms of transport may emerge from the demise of the internal combustion engine. Politicians are often blind to the numerous subtle ways in which their laws stifle changes that are desirable; in the sphere of green energy their eyes must be opened – or they must commission others to look on their behalf.

During the Second World War, decades of research into nuclear technology were compressed into a few years, with each side knowing that a nuclear bomb would bring victory. The horror of global warming far exceeds that of Nazi domination, and the urgency of developing the right means of overcoming it is no less. The decision to outlaw greenhouse gas emissions within a few years would surely stimulate an equal acceleration of human ingenuity.

5

Anti-Usury Manifesto

━━━◆•◆•◆━━━

5.1 Unite against usury

(See 1.1, 1.2, 1.3 and 1.4)

All life involves risk. So when we engage in economic activity of any kind, we cannot know the degree to which that activity will succeed or fail in its objects. Nor can we quantify risk: calculations of risk always involve projecting the past into the future, and human beings have no means of knowing whether the future will be like the past.

Usury occurs where risk is skewed, with one party taking most or all of the risk, while the other takes little or none. As a result usury is inevitably unjust – although the parties cannot know who will win or lose from the injustice. The only way for economic activity to be fair and just is for risk to be shared between the parties, both the risk of success and the risk of failure.

Unjust transactions of any kind cause wider problems in an economy. Usury in its various forms is the primary cause of economic injustice, because it arises not merely from human intention but also from inevitable human ignorance. In the modern context it causes three chronic crises. First, there is a welfare crisis: usurious taxation starves social welfare – healthcare, education and pensions – of funds. Second, there is an economic crisis: usurious forms of finance depress demand, destabilize banking and drive up unemployment. Third, there is an ecological crisis: cumulative pollution is itself a form of usury that threatens humanity's very survival.

And just as these crises have a common cause, so their solutions are connected. Solving the crisis in welfare is essential to solving the economic crisis; and solving them both is essential to solving the ecological crisis.

When people of faith across the world – Jews and Christians, Muslims and Hindus, Buddhists and Taoists – look in their scriptures and other ancient writings for guidance on economic matters, they find usury condemned as the primary economic evil. The abolition of the main forms of usury should also be the primary aim of people across the modern political spectrum. Without usury, businesses would enjoy far greater freedom, so enterprise would flourish – as those of right-wing convictions wish. Without usury, everyone willing to work would have a job, and those on lower incomes would have far better social welfare services – for which socialists of left-wing convictions have long campaigned. And without usury the hopes of environmentalists could at last be realized.

Usury – the unequal allocation of risk – is the underlying cause of three chronic crises besetting modern society: a welfare crisis, starving education, healthcare and pensions of funds; an economic crisis, destabilizing the financial system and depriving people of gainful work; and an ecological crisis, threatening humanity's survival. All major religions condemn usury; those of religious convictions should unite with those of both left-wing and right-wing political convictions in opposing usury, and thence advocating the changes necessary to solve the crises.

5.2 Trust ourselves

(See 2.1, 3.1 and 4.1)
When the state taxes our income or expenditure, it is engaged in usury. When the owners of businesses and their workers take

risks, they know that through taxation the state will take a large portion of the rewards of any success they achieve, but will carry none of the losses. So taxation transfers a share of the upside risks of business and work to the state, while leaving all the downside risks to those who take them.

As a result taxation suppresses enterprise. It causes the owners of businesses to take fewer risks. Insofar as businesses pay wages according to success, it reduces wages. It also deters individuals from starting their own businesses. This in turn lowers the rate of economic growth. So by raising the rates of tax, governments are liable to reduce the revenue they receive. And, since the loss of growth is cumulative, this loss of revenue will grow larger year-on-year.

But at the same time there is growing demand for the welfare services that modern governments provide – especially healthcare, education and pensions. As people grow richer, their demand for manufactured goods rises more slowly, while their demand for better welfare rises more quickly. And the cost of provision steadily increases, as people live longer, as new medical treatments are developed, and as staff salaries rise.

So the gap between the state's provision of welfare and people's demands grows steadily wider, with no means of closing it. Anyone opting out of state provision of healthcare and education pays twice, once through taxation and once privately – which few people can afford. Usurious taxation thus creates a paradox of care: individuals would be willing to allocate more of their income to their welfare; but, while welfare is financed through taxation, they have no means of doing this.

The primary means of resolving the paradox of care is to emulate on a larger scale the way in which, in past centuries, the extended family looked after its members. Thus people should contribute directly towards their own welfare, rather than pay through taxation. And current contributions should finance current welfare – just as in the extended family healthy adults cared for the sick and elderly and taught the young.

This implies the creation of social welfare trusts, in which people make payments month by month, and from which they receive benefits as and when they need them. Everyone would be required to belong, contributing enough to enjoy adequate welfare. People would also have the option of paying more to receive more, so expenditure on social welfare would grow in response to demand.

There could be separate trusts for healthcare, education and pensions. And, since everyone benefits from children being well educated, even those without children should contribute to an educational trust. Initially the trusts could be national or regional, developing from the existing state organizations. But soon groups should be able to establish voluntary trusts, subject to rules imposed by the state.

Some trusts would run their own hospitals and surgeries, schools and colleges. Others would finance the private purchase of healthcare and education by their members. The state would continue to monitor the quality of every institution providing social welfare.

The state would now have to raise far less in taxation. And there are other parts of public expenditure, such as the provision of roads, that could be financed by direct contributions. But the state would need to subsidize the contributions to social welfare trusts of those too poor to pay them, and also to provide such social welfare as the trusts failed to cover. And it would continue to fulfil its most basic functions of enforcing laws and defending borders.

The state should seek to raise the necessary revenue by taxing wealth whose holders have done nothing to create it. In particular it should tax inherited wealth, and also the basic value of land prior to improvements made by human effort. It should only resort to other forms of tax to the extent that taxes on unearned wealth fall short.

Taxation on income and expenditure suppresses enterprise and discourages effort, because it transfers much of the positive risks of business to the state, and hence reduces tax revenue; so public expenditure on social welfare – education, healthcare and pensions – falls far below people's demands. People should be required to contribute directly to social welfare trusts, reflecting true demand, from which they would receive benefits as needed; tax revenues for social welfare should be restricted to helping those unable to afford the full contributions.

5.3 Invest fairly

(See 2.2, 3.2 and 4.2)

When people lend and borrow money at interest, they are engaged in usury. The borrowers are obliged to pay interest and repay the principal at the times agreed. So the lenders know how they will benefit. But, if the borrower is a business, its owners cannot know whether their business will thrive, making it easy to pay the interest, or whether the business will struggle, making it hard. So the borrower contracts to carry the risk. For the lender the only risk is that the borrower defaults and the debt cannot be recovered.

When people hold money as an asset, rather than spend it, they too are engaged in usury. They are lending to society the work they performed in earning that money, and they have the right to call in that loan at any time in the future by purchasing goods and services. If the value of money is constant, they know what their money will buy. But the rest of society does not know the cost of supplying what they will buy: if productivity rises in the meantime, society gains; if it falls, society loses. So they transfer risk from themselves to society.

When people deposit money in a bank, holding it in a savings account, these two forms of financial usury fuse. The interest on the account compensates for inflation, so the value of their deposit remains constant or rises. And the bank guarantees that they can withdraw their money after a specified period of notice. Moreover, the government guarantees the bank's guarantee, because bank deposits are the main form of money and hence vital for normal economic activity. As a result, if those borrowing from the bank default in sufficiently large numbers, the government will make up the losses so the depositors' money is safe. Thus depositors transfer risk from themselves to the banks, and ultimately to society.

Wise families save money for the future, to provide for old age and sickness, and for their children and grandchildren. The paradox of care compels even greater savings; but even when it has been resolved, people will still wish to accumulate wealth. And they want much of their wealth to be safe. They may buy, directly or through investment funds, such secure assets as government bonds or debentures in large companies. Yet the sensible level of thrift in society is likely to be so high that the yields on the assets fall towards zero. So people simply hold money idly in banks, receiving enough interest to cover inflation.

As a result total demand falls below the economy's capacity to produce goods and services. And as this gap widens, so more and more of the workforce are unable to find work. Financial usury thus creates a paradox of thrift: for individuals it is beneficial to accumulate idle money, while for society as a whole it is profoundly damaging.

The banks may for a time disguise this paradox. When they lend depositors' money for businesses to invest, the money remains in circulation, so total demand remains buoyant. When they lend it to families to buy property, it also remains in circulation. But as they lend more and more of people's savings for property, they push property prices upwards. Eager to share these gains, families start borrowing more in order to buy more property than they need – larger houses and second homes. They also save less, regarding their property as their pension.

Yet this boom relies on the banks lending ever greater amounts. Once deposits fail to keep pace with the demand for loans, property prices quickly tumble – and the economy slumps. In the process numerous borrowers default, forcing governments to subsidize the banks.

Governments can boost demand by spending more than they raise in tax, borrowing the difference by issuing bonds. But they must eventually repay these debts, or else cause inflation to erode their value – which in effect steals from the lenders. So government deficits are not a permanent solution.

Resolving the paradox of care will partly resolve the paradox of thrift, since it will eliminate the major motive for thrift. Indeed, the main reason for social welfare trusts to be financed by current contributions is that they should not themselves become repositories of thrift. Moreover, it would be right to resolve the paradox of thrift only if people had reliable alternative means of providing for their future welfare. Nonetheless many will continue wishing to accumulate wealth in order to provide greater comfort for themselves and a legacy for themselves and their children.

The primary direct means of resolving the paradox of thrift, therefore, is to divide banking between deposit banks and capital banks, with the government explicitly withdrawing all guarantees. Deposit banks would administer the money that people deposited, and use a limited proportion to buy government bonds – the proportion set so that the interest on the bonds would cover the deposit banks' costs. Thus deposit banks would be perfectly safe, while deposits would fall in value by the rate of inflation.

Capital banks would provide finance for businesses and families, and pay their depositors a variable amount each year according to the returns they received less defaults. While they would keep a reserve of money to pay those wishing to withdraw their investment, they would not guarantee withdrawals. So money put into capital banks would be at risk; and it would remain largely in circulation.

In addition the central bank would continue to cause a positive and stable rate of inflation of around 2–3 per cent. This would ensure that people no longer held money as a form of saving, but only held it for a short time for normal transactions. In turn this would make it easier for the central bank to control inflation: by altering the quantity of the money it issued, the central bank would directly affect the value of transactions, nudging total demand – and hence inflation – up or down.

The paradox of thrift would thus be resolved. People could only accumulate wealth by investing fairly, sharing risk with those who used their money. And since money invested at risk remains in circulation, total demand would remain buoyant.

Secure forms of saving, in which savers transfer risk to society as a whole, reduce total demand in the economy, leaving a portion of the workforce unable to find work; and banks are the main channels of secure saving. Social welfare trusts would eliminate the need for secure savings. Banking should then be divided between deposit banks that simply administer people's money, so money would erode in value by the rate of inflation, and capital banks that invest it at risk; people would now only keep money for normal transactions, and invest all their savings in productive enterprises, thereby maintaining total demand.

5.4 Outlaw pollution

(See 2.3, 3.3 and 4.3)

When we pollute the environment in ways that accumulate, we commit the most pernicious form of usury. In particular, through its emission of greenhouse gases the present generation is passing to future generations risks of incalculable magnitude, the worst of which is that much of the planet may become uninhabitable.

Human beings across the world are now aware of these risks. We also know the principles of green energy, whereby the current energy of the sun is harnessed, either directly through turning sunlight into electricity, or indirectly through wind, waves and tides. Moreover, it seems likely that, with sufficient funds, companies could develop sustainable technologies capable of generating energy as cheaply, and perhaps even more cheaply, than using oil and coal.

Yet investing in green energy technology is highly risky. While a few companies may earn large profits, many will fail. Even the successful companies may take many years before paying any dividends to their investors. So people naturally opt for safer ways of accumulating wealth, ways that offer more immediate returns.

The outcome is that, after three or four decades of research into green energy technology, the results are meagre. There is thus an acute paradox of greenness: humanity as a whole regards the drastic reduction of greenhouse gas emissions as its highest priority, but as individuals few are willing to invest in achieving this.

The essential condition for resolving the paradox of greenness is resolving the paradoxes of thrift and care.

If people were no longer able to keep their money idle, and could accumulate wealth only by taking risks, then the funds available for developing all kinds of technologies – including green energy technologies – would increase. And if taxes were drastically reduced, thereby increasing the rewards of risk, people would become even more willing to invest. This in turn would hasten the development of green energy technologies, and so reduce the risks and enhance the potential returns, attracting even more investment.

The strongest possible government action is required. Governments should announce that at a certain date in the future, perhaps 15 years hence, they will outlaw fossil fuels, plus the other main generators of greenhouse gases – as they outlawed CFCs in the late 1980s.

This would immediately multiply the potential returns on green technology, further increasing the funds for development – as occurred with the development of alternatives to CFCs. Investors would anticipate that, as the date approached, the demand for green energy technologies would rise rapidly. So they would be eager to provide funds for any firm that might help to meet this demand. And it is likely that, by the time the ban on greenhouse gas emissions came into effect, green energy would be cheaper than fossil fuels.

Other milder forms of government sanctions, notably pollution taxes and carbon trading, have proved ineffective. Moreover, they have been bedevilled by the need for international agreement, with countries fearing that, if they acted alone, they would put themselves at an economic disadvantage. But if a single country or a group announced a ban on fossil fuels well in advance, the opposite would apply. Companies in those countries would become global leaders in the manufacture and installation of green energy technologies. And, as the cost of green energy fell below fossil fuels, so they would become major exporters.

The Manhattan Project during the Second World War proved how technological development, which otherwise might have taken decades, can be telescoped. Combating global warming is the most important war that humanity has ever waged. The advance announcement of an outright ban on the main sources of greenhouse gases offers the only realistic hope of developing the necessary technology in time.

Cumulative pollution, especially fossil fuel emissions, transfers appalling risks to future generations. While human beings know the principles of green energy, the development of economically viable technologies has been starved of funds. The division of banking would increase the funds available for such development, and the reduction of taxes would increase people's willingness to invest at such risk. Governments should then announce an absolute ban on the main forms of greenhouse gas emissions at a date 10–15 years hence; this would hugely increase the potential returns on green energy, attracting even more funds.

Epilogue

In propounding the case against usury in the preceding chapters, the teachings of the various scriptures, as well as the ideas of such figures as Aquinas, Calvin, Hume, Smith, Malthus and Keynes, have received due prominence. But there are other figures of importance that deserve explicit mention. The first discussed in this Epilogue, David Ricardo, appears for negative reasons: the case against usury depends on rebutting some of his key theories, which have played a central role in the history of economics. The other figures appear positively; the intention of calling them as intellectual witnesses is further to emphasize that those from the right, left and green corners of politics should unite with those of religious convictions in opposing usury.

1 Ricardo

In their mutual correspondence the economist David Ricardo tried to persuade Thomas Robert Malthus that his theory of excess savings was flawed. In a free economy, Ricardo believed, total savings by households would always equal the total investment that firms wished to make in plant and machinery. As a result total demand would always equal total potential supply, so every person wishing to work would find a job.

Ricardo's arguments boiled down to two basic assertions about human behaviour. First, he believed that people would not hoard money, since holding money idle offered no benefit. Instead they would hold only enough money to finance their normal day-to-day transactions. If they found themselves with more money than they needed for this purpose, they would either spend it on goods and services, or they would invest it in plant and machinery. This implies that the velocity of money circulating in the economy is constant – so total demand is exactly proportionate to the total stock of money.

Second, he believed that both the prices of goods and the wages paid to workers would rise and fall smoothly in response to changes in demand. So if the stock of money rose, pushing up total demand, prices and wages would rise proportionately; if the stock of money fell, dragging total demand downwards, prices and wages would fall. This implies that there can never be unemployment, except perhaps for a brief period. If total demand falls, forcing firms to reduce their workforce, wages will fall until they can restore their workforce.

In Ricardo's time money was based entirely on gold and silver, while the main cause of changes in the stock of money was trade imbalances. If a country had a trade surplus, with exports exceeding imports, it would import money in the form of precious metals from foreigners paying for the excess exports; if it had a trade deficit, it would export money. But this implied that trade imbalances, like unemployment, could only be temporary. Importing money as a result of a trade surplus would pull up prices and wages, making exports more expensive and imports cheaper – which in turn would reduce exports and increase imports until the trade surplus disappeared. Conversely, exporting money as a result of a trade deficit would push prices and wages down until the surplus disappeared.

Malthus never gave a clear refutation of Ricardo's arguments, which partly explains why in the succeeding century Ricardo's arguments prevailed. But Keynes did. In fact, Keynes' theory of persistent unemployment is in essence a refutation of Ricardo's two assertions about human behaviour. In the first place, Keynes believed that people do hoard money – although as an indirect consequence of the interest rate falling. So the velocity of money, far from being constant, rises or falls with the interest rate. Second, he believed that trade unions had become sufficiently strong to prevent wages from falling, even in the face of mass unemployment. So falling total demand, associated with people holding money idle, would cause unemployment to rise.

In 1956 the Chicago economist Milton Friedman, in *Studies in the Quantity Theory of Money*, presented Ricardo's views on money afresh, with some small amendments. Then in 1968, in an article in the *American Economic Review*, he renewed in a highly sophisticated fashion Ricardo's views on wages and prices. However, whereas Ricardo had assumed that wages would respond instantly to a fall in demand, Friedman acknowledged that workers would take time to adapt. Indeed, in this regard the difference between Keynes and Friedman was the length of time workers would take to adapt: Friedman believed they would do so quickly, while Keynes thought they would be slow. Friedman's views came to be known as 'monetarism'.

Recent experience suggests that wages in some economies, such as the USA and the UK, are more flexible than they were in Keynes' time. Trade unions are weaker; and, more importantly, workers are more willing to accept wage cuts in order to save their jobs, even when trade unions represent them. But it remains quite rational for workers to agree to job losses if they occur through their firms not recruiting replacements for those who retire or leave voluntarily. Indeed, this is another example of a paradox arising from usury. Existing workers transfer the risks associated with declines in total demand to new workers, including young people entering the workforce. While it is rational for individual workers to act in this way, it damages society as a whole.

Yet no degree of flexibility in wages can compensate for people hoarding money. If wages and prices were to fall in response to falling total demand, then the real value of the money in circulation would rise – the same amount of money would be worth more. So people, according to Keynes' analysis, would simply hoard more, causing total demand in the economy to fall exactly in line with wages and prices.

It follows that the crucial difference between Ricardians and Malthusians, monetarists and Keynesians, is not over the degree of flexibility in wages, but on whether and to what degree people hold money as an asset. And there can be no definitive answer, correct for all time and in all circumstances. Rather, the answer depends on the attractions of money compared with other assets. In assessing alternative assets, people will balance their likely returns, and the degree of risk.

At present fiat money is not attractive: it loses value by the rate of inflation, and central banks are generally committed to a positive rate of inflation. By contrast bank deposits are highly attractive: if depositors accept quite minimal restrictions on withdrawals, the banks pay interest that is usually higher than inflation; and the relevant government, either implicitly or explicitly, guarantees deposits. So many people are happy to hoard money in the form of bank deposits.

If, however, the banking system were divided between deposit and capital banks, and if central banks remained committed to positive inflation, bank deposits would lose their attraction, because the deposit banks would no longer be able to pay interest to match inflation. People might then, as Keynes predicted, turn to government bonds as a kind of 'near-money', making these a vehicle for hoarding. But if the government gradually bought back or redeemed its existing bonds, while restricting the issue of new bonds, then bonds could no longer serve this purpose.

The economy would thus cease to be Malthusian, and would become Ricardian – it would be monetarist instead of Keynesian. As a result, rather than suffer chronic unemployment, it would enjoy persistent full employment.

2 Fisher

The American economist Irving Fisher is best known for his mathematical formula expressing Ricardo's views about money.

In fact, he appears to have believed not only that people never hold money as an asset, but also that the amount they hold for the purpose of transactions never changes as a proportion of their annual income; so he expressed the velocity of money circulation as a constant. Friedman softened this dogma, arguing that changes in various kinds of practical arrangements – such as whether people are typically paid weekly or monthly – can alter the velocity; he concluded that it is stable, changing only slowly.

Fisher also shared Ricardo's belief in the flexibility of wages and prices in the face of changes in total demand. This led him to an insight of his own that is highly relevant to the economic crisis – one which he called 'debt-deflation'. When total demand in the economy falls, causing prices and wages to fall, the real value of debts rises, as does the interest they pay. So borrowers, both firms and households, find the burden of debt grows heavier, and they are more likely to default.

Fisher expounded this insight in *Econometrica* (1933), in the depths of the Great Depression. And debt-deflation was clearly the immediate cause of tens of thousands of firms collapsing. During the years prior to the Depression, many firms had become highly 'geared', financing their expansion largely through loans rather than issuing shares. When demand for their output started to fall, and as the prices paid by consumers also fell, they no longer had sufficient revenue for the interest payments. Their lenders concluded that there was little hope of recovery, and so foreclosed, hoping to garner some compensation from the sale of the firms' assets.

In itself the main effect of debt-deflation is to hasten the demise of firms that are already doomed. In the event of a firm selling its assets, lenders rarely receive more than a modest fraction of the money owed to them. So, if a firm falling victim to debt-deflation were viable, it would be in the interest of lenders to renegotiate the terms of their loans, taking into account changes in prices. It is reasonable to assume, therefore, that when lenders foreclose on a firm suffering debt-deflation, they regard its prospects as hopeless.

But where banks are the intermediaries between lenders and borrowers, debt-deflation becomes far more sinister. If deflation – falling prices – persists over a number of years, it will push more and more firms and households to default on their bank loans; so whether the banks renegotiate these loans or foreclose, they will incur increasing losses. Yet the banks have no means of renegotiating the terms of their deposits, which are subject to an absolute guarantee. So the gap between the banks' assets and liabilities – the loans they have made and their deposits – will grow steadily wider.

This has terrifying consequences for governments, and thence for taxpayers. Since, under the present arrangements, governments effectively guarantee banks' deposits, governments will have to spend more and more money bridging the gap between loans and deposits – until eventually the government itself becomes insolvent.

The flexibility of wages in many modern economies, with workers being willing to accept wage cuts, is widely praised as a means of mitigating the worst effects of falling total demand: it enables firms to maintain sales by reducing prices – and hence to preserve jobs. But flexible wages greatly increase the likelihood of overall deflation. Once deflation starts, people begin to expect further deflation, which makes deflation worse. Consumers delay their purchases of durable goods, anticipating that they will be able to buy them more cheaply later; so demand falls further, forcing firms to slash prices even more vigorously. And firms and workers become accustomed to paying and receiving lower wages each year. So deflationary expectations are liable to make deflation very hard to cure – just as inflationary expectations made the inflation of the 1970s and 1980s so stubborn.

When governments around the world saved the banks from collapsing in 2008, they quickly congratulated themselves for their prompt action, albeit at huge cost to their taxpayers. They imagined themselves to have awoken instantly from the nightmare of global financial collapse. But, if deflation takes hold, the nightmare will have only just begun. Since financial usury – lending at interest through the banks – is the cause of the nightmare, the abolition of financial usury will be the only means of waking from it.

3 Marx

Karl Marx was undoubtedly aware of the writings of Malthus, referring to them in several places. He agreed with Malthus that in capitalist economies total demand tends to fall below total supply, creating what he called an 'industrial reserve army' of unemployed workers. But his explanation, as expressed in *Das Kapital* (1867), was somewhat different. Marx believed that competition between firms would force them continuously to reduce their costs by substituting machinery for labour – changing the 'organic composition of capital', in Marx's peculiar phrase. The workers made redundant by this process would have less money to spend, so firms would find themselves producing more goods than they could sell. Firms would respond by cutting production, rendering even more workers redundant. Thus there would be a vicious circle in which rising unemployment itself caused unemployment to rise further.

As it stands, this analysis is wrong. New firms will tend to spring up, absorbing the workers who have been replaced by machines. And, just as technological innovation creates better machines for production, so it also creates better products for consumption, boosting total demand. But Marx was right in believing that declining total demand causes total demand to fall even further. Indeed, the circle is more vicious than Marx realized. When people see unemployment rising, they tend to save more, protecting themselves against the possibility of their own redundancy.

But Marx's most important insights concern the consequences of an expanding army of unemployed workers. The initial recruits to this army may accept their poverty with docility, comforted perhaps by the promises of religion, which Marx famously described as 'the opiate of the masses'. Eventually, however, the industrial reserve army will become so large that it will have the power to overthrow the existing political and economic order. And it will exercise this power, instituting a socialist regime in which the state owns all productive capital on behalf of the population as a whole.

Marx predicted that Britain, as the first country to industrialize, would also be the first to enjoy socialist revolution. In the event the largely agrarian economy of Russia became the cradle of socialism. Yet Marx was right to connect economic crisis with political upheaval. The Great Depression of the 1920s and 1930s bred Hitler's 'national socialism' and Mussolini's Fascism; and revolutionary parties of various ideologies attracted huge memberships in every Western country. The prospects for the present century seem scarcely less dire as unemployment rises once again, and as welfare services crumble. And it is hard to imagine that the early victims of global warming – the tens of millions whose lands are flooded by rising sea levels or reduced to deserts by decreasing rainfall – will not in some way demand reparation from those who continue to live in comfort.

As he explained in *Critique of the Gotha Programme* (1875), Marx regarded socialism as temporary, to be replaced by communism. The market economy, so he believed, engendered attitudes of selfishness and greed – 'commodity fetishism'. But a socialist economy, organized by the state for the benefit of all, would nurture a spirit of cooperation. People would then freely adopt the communist principle, 'from each according to his abilities, and to each according to his needs'. They would thus be capable of organizing for themselves productive enterprises in which everyone shared the benefits – and the state would wither away.

In fact, socialist states have proved stubbornly unwilling to wither, with the socialist elites tenaciously clinging to power;

when Russian socialism collapsed in 1991, the cause was its grotesque inefficiencies. Equally, far from nurturing virtue, socialism has tended to foster criminality, with the socialist elites using their economic power to attract bribes and to divert the profits of state enterprises to themselves.

Yet social welfare trusts would, at least in some degree, embody the principle of communism – which derives from the Bible (Acts 2.45). They would provide help for their members according to need. The members would run them on their own behalf. And, where people lacked the ability to make an adequate contribution for themselves, others through the tax system would make up the shortfall. In the meantime, deprived of its functions in providing social welfare, the state would wither to a fraction of its present size.

4 Paine

During the Industrial Revolution several writers advocated the education of the poor, and proposed schemes for public subsidies.

Adam Smith, for example, feared that work in the new factories was so repetitive, and so devoid of skill, that it would dull the workers' brains. He regarded the education of workers' children as an antidote, so that in adulthood they would be able to reflect on their own existence. However, he strongly opposed direct provision by the state, since the lack of competition would lead to poor standards of teaching and inefficiency of administration. Instead, he proposed imitating the system in place at Glasgow University, where the state provided the buildings, while the pupils or their parents paid for the teachers – so a teacher's income would depend on the number of pupils he could attract. The state would also decree a minimum standard of education that every child should receive.

It was Thomas Paine, however, who first recognized the direct economic benefits of education. Born in England, he emigrated to America in 1774, where he became a leading proponent of

American independence; returning to England in 1787, he strongly supported the French Revolution. In 1791 he published *The Rights of Man*, his vision of a just and free society.

Paine believed that when young men started work, they were often held back by their illiteracy and innumeracy. Even those undertaking apprenticeships, in which they learnt complex skills, would become much more productive, and hence earn more money, if they could follow written instructions and perform basic mathematical calculations. But, like Smith, he abhorred the idea of teachers being employed by the state, fearing not only that they would be lax, but also that they would indoctrinate children with state propaganda. Instead, parents should choose the school to which they sent their children, and pay the fees directly. For its part the government should help parents by freeing them from the obligation to pay taxes; to very poor parents it should offer a direct allowance. Beyond this the government should confine itself to checking that every child attended school, and that every school provided adequate instruction.

Half a century later, in *On Liberty* (1859), John Stuart Mill echoed Paine's views almost precisely. Mill believed that parents had a duty to educate their children, and that the state should enforce this duty. But, suspicious of the state using schools to control children's minds, he too wanted schools to operate independently, with the state subsidizing the fees of poorer families. His main refinement was to suggest regular public examinations to monitor the standard of education that each school provided.

In almost every country across the world the government has long accepted the role of ensuring that every child is educated. But few governments have been able to resist the temptation of running schools themselves. Of course, governments generally deny any attempt to use schools as vehicles of indoctrination. Yet in determining the curriculum that schools follow, the state cannot help promulgating a particular set of values; and teachers, as employees of the state, inevitably tend to share those values. More obviously, educational systems operated by the state are generally inefficient and wasteful, and they lack the variety of style and method that independence would promote. So their standards, especially in areas of social and economic deprivation, are often low.

The proposals contained in this book for social welfare trusts are mainly directed at increasing the money spent on education, as well as on healthcare and pensions. The trusts would also take the provision of education and healthcare out of the hands of the state, and vest it in such institutions as the trusts and their members saw fit. Thus efficiency would also increase, and there would be greater opportunity for innovation. Surely, therefore, such arrangements are what Paine and Mill would be advocating if they were alive today.

Unfortunately in the intervening decades there has been an inversion of political beliefs that has caused a strange ambivalence to Paine and Mill. In their time they were both regarded as radicals, even revolutionaries, whose ideas inspired those of left-wing convictions but were repugnant to conservatives. Yet now their views on education appeal to those on the right wing, while left-wingers heartily reject them. Indeed, for many people on the left of politics, it is an article of faith that the state alone should educate the young, as well as treat the sick.

This political muddle offers a vivid illustration of an underlying theme of this book: that, in facing the major challenges of our time, people across the political spectrum can remain true to their intellectual traditions, while standing on common ground. And, although Paine and Mill were both atheists, those of religious beliefs should share that ground.

5 Gandhi

Mohandas Gandhi – commonly given the title 'Mahatma', meaning 'great soul' – is a rare example of an ascetic committed to living frugally, who was also interested in economics. His formal training was in law, and as a young man he practised as a lawyer in South Africa. But it was largely on economic grounds that he came to advocate India's independence from Britain. India, he argued, had become an economic slave of Britain, selling its raw materials to Britain's factories and then buying back their goods; this had undermined the traditional Indian economy, impoverishing its people. Thus India could only restore its prosperity by retaining its raw materials and producing its own goods; and this would require freedom from British rule.

At one level, therefore, Gandhi was opposing Ricardo's ideas on international trade. In his theory of comparative advantage Ricardo argued that each country gains by specializing in producing goods with the lowest relative costs, and then trading those goods for cheap goods produced elsewhere. This requires workers within a country to be mobile, both geographically and in the skills they acquire. Gandhi by contrast believed that labour was immobile – and should remain immobile. He pointed in particular to the manufacture of textiles.

Prior to British rule the spinning and weaving of cotton had been a part-time occupation, undertaken in cottages on simple spinning-wheels and handlooms. So it provided families in India's villages with an additional source of income over and above what they earned from growing crops; this had enabled them to enjoy a reasonable degree of material comfort. As a result, when India began sending its raw cotton to the mills of Lancashire in England, the rural families had no means of seeking alternative work without also abandoning their lands, and hence risking starvation. So they were cast into permanent poverty – and Gandhi made the spinning-wheel the symbol of Indian independence.

The rapid economic growth enjoyed by India since the early 1990s would seem at last to prove Ricardo right and Gandhi wrong. Under British rule, and more especially in the decades following independence, India's economy was weighed down by all kinds of regulations and restrictions. But once the government began to lift these burdens, all kinds of new businesses and industries began springing up in India's towns and cities, offering jobs to the young men and women from the surrounding countryside. There remain huge swathes of rural India still mired in poverty. But India now seems to be experiencing an economic transformation, equivalent to the Industrial Revolution in Britain two centuries ago, that promises eventually to lift the living standards of even the remotest village.

Yet Gandhi was actually making a deeper point. In his voluminous writings and speeches (for example, *Khadi*, 1955) he frequently conceded the capacity of a dynamic, mobile economy, of the kind advocated by Ricardo, to increase the quantity of goods that people produce and consume. But in his view the quality of their lives would be progressively worsened. Gandhi's vision was of local communities that were to a large degree self-sufficient, producing goods and services largely for themselves. People would typically undertake several different tasks in the course of each day, week and year, finding satisfaction in practising the various skills that each task required. The communities would also run schools and clinics to which every family would contribute a substantial portion of its time and income. And, since the communities would have a direct interest in their own natural environment, they would ensure that its fauna and flora thrived.

Gandhi called his vision *panchayat raj* – *panchayat* referring to the five elders who traditionally oversaw the affairs of an Indian village. And there is no doubting its attractions. Indeed, Gandhi was unconsciously echoing the description of communism given by Karl Marx in *The German Ideology* (1845). But Marx understood that communism would only function successfully if people had already abandoned greed and self-interest in favour of generosity and cooperation. While Marx hoped that a period of socialism would achieve this, Gandhi seems simply to have trusted the essential goodness of the human heart.

Babu Patwardhan, a follower of Gandhi, believed that *panchayat raj* could be achieved only if its structures were sufficiently robust to withstand human badness. Indeed, in *Chalanashuddhi* (1967) he embraced Adam Smith's conviction that the best economic structures are those that channel human desires for the good of all, whether those desires are generous or greedy. So his practical proposals for the abolition of usury – on which the proposals in this book are ultimately based – were in effect an attempt to adapt the means advocated by Smith to the ends advocated by Gandhi.

And it is here that Gandhi's economic vision has continuing value. Orthodox economics judges the success of an economy by the quantity of goods and services it produces, measured as its 'gross domestic product' (GDP). But GDP conspicuously excludes any assessment of an economy's impact on the environment, and also any indication of the security of people's employment and the satisfaction they derive from their work. Equally, it values healthcare and education purely by the amount of taxation spent on them, not by the benefits that people derive. Gandhi implicitly urged us to complement quantitative measurements with qualitative judgments, in which welfare, work and the environment are the main foci.

The proposals contained in this book would not reduce the rate at which GDP increases. On the contrary, by ensuring full employment, and by encouraging investment in green energy technology, they would tend to increase it. But their main effect would be vastly to improve the economy by Gandhi's qualitative standards.

6 Schrödinger

Most Western philosophers, and most Westerners who reflect on the nature of the universe, are 'physicalists': they regard the universe as entirely physical, and consider that mental phenomena arise out of particular kinds of physical entities. Thus our consciousness – our thoughts and feelings – somehow emerges out of the grey matter of our brains. No philosopher or scientist has yet provided a satisfactory account of how minds emerge from brains; some, such as Colin McGinn in *Problems in Philosophy* (1993), have argued that the human mind is inherently incapable of understanding its relationship with its brain. So physicalism is more a dogma than a theory.

By extension most thoughtful Westerners are also determinists. Since the universe is physical, so they believe, it must function according to physical laws. Thus each state of the universe follows inexorably from the previous state; and all future states are contained in the present state. This implies that our uncertainty about the future arises from our ignorance, and that, if we had sufficient information, we could predict the future with total accuracy. It also follows that free will is an illusion. Again no philosopher has provided a satisfactory explanation for this illusion, or even explained what function consciousness might perform; in a determinist universe brains are merely machines, analogous to computers. So, like physicalism, determinism is more a dogma than a theory.

In the early decades of the last century, however, the discoveries of quantum mechanics cast doubt on both physicalism and determinism, although philosophers have been slow to grasp their potential implications. The central insight of quantum mechanics, which can be fairly simply demonstrated, is that at the sub-atomic level particles are also waves. And the central implication for human knowledge is contained in the 'uncertainty principle', first stated in 1927 by one of the pioneers of quantum mechanics, Werner Heisenberg: we can know either the location of a sub-atomic entity, or its momentum, but not both. In other words, we can perceive sub-atomic entities as either particles with a specific location, or as waves with a specific wavelength and frequency, but we cannot perceive both a particle and its corresponding wave at the same time.

This leads to a profound conundrum about the relationship between the universe and our perception of it. In our daily existence we perceive objects with specific locations; and these objects comprise billions of sub-atomic particles. So it would seem that, once human consciousness becomes involved, the waves 'de-cohere', becoming particles. Some of the quantum pioneers, including Erwin Schrödinger, concluded that consciousness itself turns an almost infinite number of possible universes into an actual universe. Of course, to most quantum physicists – who are committed to a physicalist view of the universe – this idea is utterly repugnant; but they remain mystified by de-coherence. Schrödinger, however, in works such as *What is Life?* (1944), looked eastwards, to the ancient Hindu philosophy of Advaita Vedanta, for an alternative to physicalism and determinism.

Advaita Vedanta argues that the universe cannot be purely physical, because it undoubtedly contains the phenomenon of consciousness, which is not physical. It also argues that the universe cannot contain two separate forms of existence, physical and mental, since they cannot connect: physical existence cannot have mental properties, and mental existence cannot have physical properties. So it concludes that the universe is purely mental – it is a huge mind, of which individual minds are small fragments – and that the physical appearance of things is a veil (*maya*).

Schrödinger speculated that the basic element of the universal mind is waves, so that the universe is a vast 'wave function'. The universe then chooses at each moment a particular solution to the wave function in which waves becomes particles. This implies that there are two quite distinct types of causality in the universe. First, there is a basic causality relating to waves and their interaction; this conforms to laws that are immutable, so it is deterministic. Second, there is causality arising from the choices made by the universal mind, including the individual minds within it; this is free, and hence impossible to predict.

The notion of the universe as mental – sometimes called 'metaphysical idealism' – is by no means confined to Hinduism.

The Stoics of ancient Greece seem to have propounded a similar idea, as did the great Jewish philosopher, Benedict Spinoza. Although both the Old and the New Testament are largely devoid of philosophical speculation, each contains at least one passage suggesting that the foundation of the universe is mental: Proverbs 8.11–31 and John 1.1–5 – the latter of which, via Philo of Alexandria, was probably influenced by Stoic ideas. Within Christian history metaphysical idealism is expressed most clearly, both philosophically and poetically, within the Celtic tradition – as, for example, in the writings of Eriugena. And, while he argued for dualism of mind and matter, there is an intriguing hint that the universe is mental in the works of René Descartes: in his *Meditations* (1641) he suggested that the universe consists only of geometric shapes; and in *Geometry* (1637) he showed that geometry is reducible to algebra – which is a purely mental construct.

Most economists, at least in their professional activities, share the twin dogmas of physicalism and determinism. They believe that human beings behave, at least in their economic activities, according to laws, expressed in equations; and they use these equations to create models of how economies will evolve through time. So they imagine that, by applying current economic data to their models, they can predict how economies will perform over the coming months and years. Moreover, they tell politicians that, by using particular policies to influence economic behaviour, they can change that performance in particular ways.

Economists recognize that their equations may not be entirely correct, so their predictions may not be wholly accurate; as a result they often attach probabilities to their predictions, based on the degree to which past predictions have been wrong. But they ascribe any faults in their equations to lack of information about the laws of economics, convinced that with better information their predictions would be more accurate. Hence they think that risks arise from ignorance – and so, to the degree to which greater knowledge can be acquired, that risk can be reduced.

But quantum mechanics, by showing that the universe is inherently uncertain, proves that no amount of information and knowledge can reveal the future. And metaphysical idealism asserts that human beings are inherently free, so equations can never describe their behaviour, nor can probability factors express the degree of our ignorance about their behaviour. Hence economists creating their models, and politicians following their guidance, are akin to the people of ancient Babylon building a tower to the sky, in the hope that they might see and control the world (Genesis 11.1–9). Of course, economic behaviour is reasonably consistent from one year to the next, with people generally responding to similar circumstances in similar ways. So economists can make general predictions about the effects of particular policies – indeed, the present book is full of such predictions. And economists can often perceive quite clearly where risks lie – the present book is full of such perceptions. But the monumental failure to predict the events of 2007/08 – a failure that even Queen Elizabeth II was overheard to lament – bears witness to the folly of the towers of equations that economists labour to construct.

The inherent uncertainty of the economic future is the fundamental reason why usury – the unequal allocation of risk – must necessarily be immoral. It is also the reason why the reduction and abolition of usury will generally be benign. Just as people respond to the absence of risk by being thoughtless or even reckless in their actions, so they naturally respond to risk by being more careful, thinking through the potential consequences of what they do. So when all the parties to a transaction share the risks, they will all take care to ensure the best possible outcome.

If we all shared the risks involved in welfare, we should take care to ensure our welfare provision was ample. If we all shared the risks of creating wealth for the future, we should take care to ensure our wealth was genuine. And, most importantly, if we all shared the risks of developing green technologies, we should all take care in bequeathing a healthy planet to our descendants.

Glossary of terms and people

*Note: An asterisk * beside a term indicates that it is defined elsewhere in the Glossary.*

Advaita Vedanta: the most influential school of Hindu philosophy. It teaches that in reality the universe is a mind, and that the physical appearance of things is a veil (*maya*). Within the West this view, sometimes known as 'metaphysical idealism', is associated with the Dutch-Jewish philosopher Benedict Spinoza (1632–77).

Aquinas, Thomas (*c.*1225–74): priest, theologian and philosopher from Sicily, who taught at the University of Paris. His ideas have exerted a major influence on the teaching of the Roman Catholic Church.

Bentham, Jeremy (1748–1832): English philosopher and political theorist. He believed that human happiness may be measured as pleasure minus pain; he is famous for the utility principle, which states that governments should pursue policies that bring the greatest happiness to the greatest number. He was an avowed atheist.

Bond: a form of long-term debt in which the annual payments by the borrower to the lenders are fixed. Both governments and public companies issue bonds. The annual payments generally reflect the prevailing long-term interest* rate at the time of the bond's issue, with a premium for the perceived risk of the borrower defaulting on (not paying) the annual payment or the final repayment.

Callendar, Guy Stewart (1898–1964): English engineer and amateur meteorologist, who pioneered the idea that carbon dioxide is a greenhouse gas,* causing global warming.*

87

Calvin, John (1509–64): French theologian who was one of the major Protestant reformers. He was especially successful in reforming the church in Geneva, where he also exerted a strong influence in economic and civic affairs.

Capital bank: a term coined in this book to refer to a bank that provides finance for firms and households, and where the value of the money invested in it may rise or fall according to the returns the bank obtains. It is distinct from a modern commercial bank, which guarantees the amount people put in it, with the central bank* in practice underwriting that guarantee. It is also distinct from a modern investment bank, which trades in shares* and bonds.*

Central bank: a bank that manages a particular currency, supervising the issue of fiat money* in that currency. The government – or, in the case of the euro, the group of participating governments – lays down the rules by which the central bank operates. The central bank typically also supervises the banking system in its currency area, while the government authorizes and provides funds for the guaranteeing of deposits at banks.

Debenture: a type of bond* issued by a public company. The company's debentures, and also its shares,* can generally be traded on a stock exchange.

Deflation: falling prices of goods and services in an economy. It is the opposite of inflation,* and is also sometimes called 'negative inflation'.

Deposit bank: a term coined in this book for a bank that takes deposits, and either holds them as fiat money* or uses them to buy government bonds.* A deposit bank guarantees the deposits without any need for the central bank* to underwrite the guarantee. Elsewhere in economic literature deposit banks are variously called 'safe banks' and 'narrow banks'.

Depression: a prolonged period when total demand* is weak, causing sustained high unemployment.*

Fiat money: money whose value derives from the government declaring that it may be used to settle all debts. Typically it takes the form of paper notes and coins made from cheap metal.

Fisher, Irving (1867–1947): American economist who argued that the money supply determines the level of average prices, and hence whether there is inflation* or deflation.* He also analysed the dangers of deflation to businesses.

Friedman, Milton (1912–2006): American economist who advocated free markets. He argued that controlling the money supply directly determines total demand in an economy, and that flexible wages, moving down as well as up in response to changes in demand, preserve full employment.

Gandhi, 'Mahatma' (1869–1948): the leader of the movement for the political independence of India from the UK, and a proponent of *panchayat raj*, by which local communities would have a high degree of economic independence. His first name was Mohandas, and he acquired the title 'Mahatma', meaning 'great soul', as a mark of respect.

George, Henry (1839–1897): American writer and political activist, who believed that all land should be regarded as common property, and argued that poverty could be eliminated by imposing a tax on the 'unimproved value' of all privately owned land.

Global warming: long-term rise in the temperature of the earth's surface owing to emissions of greenhouse gases.*

Greenhouse gases: gases in the atmosphere that absorb and emit radiation in the thermal infrared range. Excessive emissions of greenhouse gases, through human activity, are thought to be causing global warming,* by which the surface of the earth is rising in temperature through a process analogous to, although different from, the heating of a greenhouse by sunlight. The main greenhouse gases are carbon dioxide and methane.

Hume, David (1711–76): Scottish philosopher, who was an empiricist, believing that all knowledge derives from the senses.

He propounded the 'riddle of induction', that it is fallacious to ascribe a probability to particular future events on the basis of past experience. He was an atheist, on the grounds that theological beliefs cannot be verified by the senses.

Income elasticity of demand: the change in the demand for a good or service in response to a change in people's income. Most goods have positive income elasticity, in that people demand more as their income rises; some goods, such as healthcare, appear to have strongly positive elasticity. Other goods have negative income elasticity, in that people buy more as their income falls; such goods are popular during a depression.*

Inflation: rising prices of goods and services in an economy. Inflation is usually measured as the percentage by which prices on average have risen over the course of a year, ironing out the effects of seasonal fluctuations. So the figure for inflation in a given month refers to the percentage by which prices have risen over the previous 12 months.

Interest: the fee paid on a loan by the borrower to the lender. Interest is usually expressed as a percentage of the amount borrowed, known as the interest rate, to be paid annually. The short-term interest rate, payable on loans taken only for a short period, is generally lower than the long-term interest rate.

Investment: the amount spent on goods, such as plant and machinery, that will help to produce more goods and services in the future.

Keynes, John Maynard (1883–1946): English economist who analysed why and how mature economies typically have savings* in excess of investment,* leading to depression.* He argued that governments could alleviate depression in the short term by spending more than they tax, borrowing the difference, but could not continue such policies in the long term.

Laffer curve: a diagram showing the relationship between tax rates and tax revenues, named after the American economist Arthur Laffer who popularized it. The vertical axis shows tax revenues, and the horizontal axis shows tax rates. When tax rates are 0 per cent, tax revenues are zero; they are also zero when tax rates are 100 per cent, because there is no incentive to work. The curve is thus a hump, with tax revenues being maximized at a tax rate somewhere between 0 per cent and 100 per cent.

Malthus, Thomas Robert (1766–1834): English economist who predicted that the human population will always tend to grow faster than its ability to feed itself, and that industrial economies will typically have excess savings* leading to depression*. He is believed to have been the first person employed as an economist, teaching political economy at Haileybury; he was also an Anglican clergyman.

Mandeville, Bernard (1670–1733): philosopher and satirist, with a particular interest in economic issues, who grew up in the Netherlands and settled in London. He argued that the private virtue of thrift leads to the public vices of poverty and idleness.

Marx, Karl (1818–83): philosopher and political economist, and prophet of communism, who grew up in Germany and settled in London. He predicted that unemployed workers would lead a revolution to overthrow the capitalist market economy of the kind analysed by Adam Smith,* replacing it with socialism, which in turn would lead to communism.

Mill, John Stuart (1806–72): English political philosopher who emphasized the importance of liberty in society, arguing that a society with freedom of expression and action will be more creative and productive than one with state controls. While he recognized the responsibility of the state in ensuring all children are educated, he opposed state-run schools, believing that the state would use them as a means of controlling ideas.

Minsky, Hyman (1919–96): American economist, often described as 'post-Keynesian', who argued that banks tend to lend excess savings recklessly, leading to periodic financial crises.

Muhammad (*c.*570–632): the founder of Islam, from Mecca on the Arabian peninsula, who claimed to receive revelations from Allah (God), later compiled as the Qu'ran.* Muslims, the followers of Islam, also treat the Hadith, which are collections of Muhammad's sayings, as authoritative.

Paine, Thomas (1737–1809): English political writer and campaigner, who supported and guided the American Revolution, and later played an active role in the French Revolution.

Pollution: side-effect of some human activity on the environment. Some forms of pollution, such as noise, do not accumulate, whereas other forms of pollution, usually above a certain level, tend to accumulate. The most significant cumulative forms of pollution are the greenhouse gases.*

Qu'ran: the scriptures of Islam. Muslims believe that Allah (God), through the angel Gabriel, made a series of revelations to Muhammad* between 610 CE and his death in 632 CE. These revelations were then compiled to form the Qu'ran.

Ricardo, David (1772–1823): English economist, strongly influenced by Adam Smith,* who argued in favour of free international trade, and also that capitalist economies are self-correcting, ensuring full employment. He was also a very successful stockbroker, and became a Member of Parliament. He was raised as a Jew, and converted to the Unitarian form of Christianity.

Risk: the range of possible outcomes of an activity. In economic activities the 'upside risk' is the possibility that an outcome might be better than expected, while the 'downside risk' is the possibility that the outcome might be worse.

Saving: the proportion of income, after payment of tax, not spent on goods and services for consumption. A household may 'dis-save', in that it spends more on consumption than its current income, financing it through past savings, as with a pension, or through borrowing. In common parlance saving is often called 'investment',* but in economics they are quite distinct.

Schrödinger, Erwin (1887–1961): Austrian physicist who was one of the pioneers of quantum mechanics, and who sought to explain its mysteries through the Hindu philosophy of Advaita Vedanta.*

Shares: the means of owning a company. In proportion to the number of shares that each holds, the shareholders receive the company's profits as 'dividends', and they elect directors to run the company on their behalf. Large public companies typically raise funds from the public by issuing a mixture of shares and debentures,* both of which can generally be traded through a stock exchange. They raise additional funds through borrowing from banks.

Smith, Adam (1723–90): Scottish economist who first analysed clearly how free markets work. He argued that self-interest, through the 'invisible hand' of the market, leads to prosperity for all. He was also a moral philosopher, arguing that human 'moral sentiments' should guide conduct.

Tariff: a tax levied on imports, typically a percentage of the imports' value. A tariff may apply to a specific type of good; the purpose of such tariffs is usually to protect domestic firms producing that good. Or a tariff may apply to all imports; its purpose is usually to reduce overall imports, and thereby boost total demand.*

Total demand: the total demand for goods and services in an economy. It is often called 'aggregate demand' or 'aggregate expenditure'. It is the sum of consumption, investment,* government expenditure, and exports minus imports.

Unemployment: a measure of the number of people willing and able to work at a reasonable rate of pay, but who are unable to find work. There are various ways of measuring unemployment, none of which is wholly satisfactory. A better measure of whether it is becoming easier or harder to find work is the number of people with jobs: if this number is falling, work is almost undoubtedly becoming harder to find.

Bibliography

Aquinas, Thomas. *Summa Theologica* (1265–74). Available via Amazon in 5 vols at £144, or downloadable in sections from the general website of the Dominicans (Order of Preachers) at <www.op.org/summa>.

Calvin, John. *De Usuris Responsum* (1545). This essay, translated as A Thesis on Usury, may be downloaded from <www.scribd.com/doc/14504769/A-Thesis-on-Usury>.

Cato, Marcus Porcius. *De Re Rustica* (*c.*200 BCE). Translated as *On Agriculture*, published by Harvard University Press in 1979, available through <www.amazon.com>.

Club of Rome (Donella H. Meadows, Dennis L. Meadows, Jorgen Randers, William W. Behrens III). *The Limits to Growth* (1972). Universe Books. For an updated version see <www.context.org/ICLB/IC32/Meadows.htm>.

Dante Alighieri. *The Divine Comedy* (1308–21). Oxford: Oxford World's Classics, new edn 1998.

Descartes, René. *Geometry* (1637). Translated from the French and Latin by David Eugene Smith and Marcia L. Latham, Dover Publications Inc., 1954, available through <www.amazon.co.uk>.

Descartes, René. *Meditations and Other Metaphysical Writings* (1641). London: Penguin Classics, 2003.

Fisher, Irving. 'The Debt-Deflation Theory of Great Depressions' (1933). *Econometrica*, Vol.1, pp. 337–357. This is the journal of the international Econometric Society, and is available from the Department of Economics, Princeton University, NJ 08544-1021, USA (see <www.econometricsociety.org> for information on downloading).

Friedman, Milton. *Studies in the Quantity Theory of Money* (1956), Chicago, IL: University of Chicago Press.

Friedman, Milton. 'The role of monetary policy', *American Economic Review*, Pittsburgh, PA (<aeaweb.org>), March 1968.

Gandhi, M. K. *Khadi: why and how*. Ahmedabad, India: Navajivan Press, 1955.

George, Henry. *Progress and Poverty* (1879). Can be downloaded from the Online Library of Liberty at <http://oll.libertyfund.org>.

Goodman, Nelson. 'The New Problem of Induction'. Article in *Fact, Fiction and Forecast* (1983). Cambridge, MA: Harvard University Press.

Hume, David. *An Enquiry Concerning Human Understanding* (1748). Mineola, NY: Dover Philosophical Classics, 2004.

Keynes, John Maynard. *The General Theory of Employment, Interest and Money* (1936). Loughton, Essex: Prometheus Books UK, reprinted 1997.

Lomborg, Bjorn. *Cool It! The skeptical environmentalist's guide to global warming*. London: Marshall Cavendish Editions/Cyan, 2007.

Malthus, Thomas Robert. *An Essay on the Principle of Population* (1798). May be read on screen at <www.esp.org/books/malthus/population/malthus.pdf>.

Malthus, Thomas Robert. *Principles of Political Economy* (1820). New York: Adamant Media Corporation, reprinted 2001. Available via <www.amazon.co.uk> or in a facsimile edition via <www.elibron.com>.

Mandeville, Bernard and E. J. Hundert. *The Fable of the Bees and Other Writings* (1714). Indianapolis, IN: Hackett Publishing Company, reprinted 1997; or sections may be read via <www.books.google.co.uk/books>.

Marx, Karl. *Critique of the Gotha Program* (1875). Rockville, MD: Wildside Press, reprinted 2008.

Marx, Karl. *Das Kapital* (1867). An abridged and translated version, *Capital*, edited by David McLellan, is available from Oxford: Oxford World's Classics, 2008.

McGinn, Colin. *Problems in Philosophy: The limits of enquiry*. Oxford: WileyBlackwell, 1993.

Mill, John Stuart. *On Liberty* (1859). London: Penguin Classics, reprinted edition including *The Subjection of Women* in 2006.

Minsky, Hyman P. *The Financial Instability Hypothesis (Working Paper)* (1978). Out of print and limited availability even through

Amazon, but may be available via the Jerome Levy Economics
Institute of Bard College, PO Box 5000, Annandale-on-Hudson,
NY 12504-5000 (<www.levy.org>).

Paine, Thomas. *The Rights of Man* (1791). Oxford: Oxford World's
Classics, republished with other writings from Paine in 2008.

Patwardhan, Appa. *Chalanashuddhi, or, Nature Forging Towards
Sarvodaya*. Ahmedabad, India: Navajivan House, 1967.

Pigou, A. C. *The Economics of Welfare* (1920). Edison, NJ:
Transaction Publishers, new edition 2001.

Ricardo, David. *On the Principles of Political Economy and Taxation*
(1817). Amherst, New York: Prometheus Books, reprinted 1996,
or download from <http://socserv2.socsci.mcmaster.ca/~econ/
ugcm/3ll3/ricardo/prin/index.html>.

Sandel, Michael. *Democracy's Discontents* (1996). Cambridge, MA:
Harvard University Press, reprinted 1998.

Schrödinger, Erwin. *What is Life?* (1944). Cambridge: Cambridge
University Press, reprinted 1992 in an edition including *Mind
and Matter* and *Autobiographical Sketches*.

Schumpeter, Joseph A. *Capitalism, Socialism and Democracy* (1942).
London: Routledge, reprinted 1994.

Smith, Adam. *An Inquiry into the Nature and Causes of the Wealth
of Nations* (1776). Oxford: Oxford World's Classics republished
in an abridged edition as *Wealth of Nations*, 2008.

Smith, Adam. *The Theory of Moral Sentiments* (1759). Cambridge:
Cambridge University Press, reprinted 2002.

Stern, Nicholas. *The Stern Review of the Economics of Climate
Change* ('The Stern Report') (2006). An Executive Summary
of this may be downloaded from the website of HM Treasury
(<hon-treasury.gov.uk>).

Stern, Nicholas. 'Time for a green industrial revolution', *New
Scientist*, 21 January 2009.

Tawney, R. H. *Religion and the Rise of Capitalism* (1926). Out of
print but still available via <www.amazon.co.uk>.